The Cognitive Behavioral Therapy Workbook *for* Personality Disorders

A STEP-BY-STEP PROGRAM

JEFFREY C. WOOD, PSY.D.

New Harbinger Publications, Inc.

Distributed in Canada by Raincoast Books

Copyright © 2010 by
New Harbinger Publications, Inc.
5674 Shattuck Avenue
Oakland, CA 94609
www.newharbinger.com

Acquired by Tesilya Hanauer; Cover design by Amy Shoup;
Edited by Kayla Sussell; Text design by Tracy Marie Carlson

Library of Congress Cataloging-in-Publication Data

Wood, Jeffrey C.
  The cognitive behavioral therapy workbook for personality disorders : a step-by-step program / Jeffrey C. Wood.
    p. cm.
  Includes bibliographical references.
  ISBN 978-1-57224-648-5
  1. Personality disorders. 2. Cognitive therapy. I. Title.
  RC554.W66 2010
  616.89'1425--dc22

                       2009052768

21   20   19

10   9   8   7   6   5

To all sentient beings who are unhappy or suffering: May you soon find relief.

Contents

PART I
Understanding Personality Disorders

CHAPTER 1
What Are Personality Disorders?

CHAPTER 2
The Eleven Personality Disorders

CHAPTER 3
Cognitive Behavioral Therapy for Personality Disorders.

PART II
Specific Cognitive Therapy Skills

CHAPTER 4
Get Reactivated in Life

PART III
Post-Treatment Care

Acknowledgments

I am grateful to the following psychologists, psychiatrists, therapists, researchers, and counselors whose compassion, hard work, and dedication made this workbook possible: Aaron Beck, Albert Ellis, Arthur Freeman, Denise Davis, James Pretzer, A. John Rush, Brian Shaw, Gary Emery, Bridget Grant, Christine Padesky, Dennis Greenberger, Donald Meichenbaum, Matthew McKay, Martha Davis, Patrick Fanning, Elizabeth Eshelman, Edmund Bourne, Jeffrey Young, Marsha Linehan, Edmund Jacobson, Thomas D'Zurilla, Alex Osborn, G. Alan Marlatt, Judith Gordon, Judith Beck, the contributing editors of the *Diagnostic and Statistical Manual of Mental Disorders*, and the dozens of others named in the references of this book.

In addition, I would like to thank my copy editor, Kayla Sussell, for making this book much better.

Introduction

Congratulations on getting this book for yourself or someone you care about. I can only imagine how challenging it must have been to admit that you have a problem and then to seek help for it. Hopefully, *The Cognitive Behavioral Therapy Workbook for Personality Disorders* will provide you with the skills you need to build a healthier, more satisfying life.

Most likely, you picked up this book because someone such as a psychologist or psychiatrist told you that you have a "personality disorder." This isn't a very flattering thing to say to someone. Clearly, this label wasn't created by anyone who was actually suffering with one of these difficult and painful problems. If it had been, the person certainly would have picked a more compassionate and appropriate label, one like "dysfunctional habit" or "troublesome interpersonal style." Understandably, no one wants to be told that he or she has a personality disorder, and I can certainly appreciate why the name alone might prevent you from reading this book. As a consequence, part of the challenge while writing it has been figuring out how to help you with your problem without scaring you away at the same time.

As you may already know, the names of the disorders discussed in this workbook often sound more judgmental than helpful. For example, narcissistic personality disorder, avoidant personality disorder, and dependent personality disorder sound insensitive or insulting to many people. In some ways, these inappropriate names probably say more about the frustration of the early mental health "experts" who failed to provide successful treatments than they do about the pain of those who were struggling with the symptoms.

Similarly, other labels give the patients who've been diagnosed with them absolutely no information about the nature of their problems. For example, schizoid personality disorder, schizotypal personality disorder, and borderline personality disorder can sound baffling, and unless you understand Greek or are an avid reader of old medical journals, you probably have no idea what these terms means. ("Schizo" means "split," by the way, and refers to splitting away from other people, while "borderline" refers to an old belief that patients with this problem were on the borderline of being psychotic.) Unfortunately, many of these names have endured and are now used in the American Psychiatric Association's official handbook of mental health problems known as the *Diagnostic and Statistical Manual of Mental Disorders*, now in its fourth edition.

With this in mind, I have attempted to be both accurate and compassionate while writing this book. However, some readers will still be bothered by the labels and descriptions that I've used, and I can't say that I blame them. However, I hope that the labels and descriptions won't stop you from getting the help you need to improve your life, fix your relationships, and end your suffering. Because no matter what name is given to these problems, it doesn't change the fact that you and millions of people like you are struggling and don't know what to do about it.

Throughout this workbook I'll encourage you to think about your life in new ways. So starting right now, instead of thinking of your personality disorder as one, very large problem that dominates all aspects of your life, I encourage you to think about it as a group of ineffective habits. Right now you use several long-standing habits that don't work, but luckily, there's a treatment called cognitive behavioral therapy (CBT) that will show you how to change those ineffective habits—one at a time.

HOW TO USE THIS WORKBOOK

Most readers will want to start at the beginning of this workbook and work through its chapters in order, since many of the skills build on one another. However, if you're working with a mental health care professional or you are using this workbook only to learn a few specific skills, use the descriptions below to guide you.

Part I, Understanding Personality Disorders, will teach you basic information about personality disorders and cognitive behavioral therapy:

- Chapter 1, What Are Personality Disorders? will help you identify the personality disorder you're suffering with by providing descriptions of other people's symptoms who are struggling with the disorder too.

- Chapter 2, The Eleven Personality Disorders, will provide you with more specific information about your personality disorder, including its symptoms, the official diagnostic criteria, and other related problems.

- Chapter 3, Cognitive Behavioral Therapy for Personality Disorders, will introduce you to a very effective treatment for personality disorders called cognitive behavioral therapy. Cognitive behavioral therapy will help you examine the way your thoughts, feelings, and behaviors all contribute to the problems you experience.

Part II, Specific Cognitive Therapy Skills, will teach you techniques that will help you cope with your problems more effectively and change many of your habits.

- In chapter 4, Get Reactivated in Life, you'll learn how to schedule both pleasurable and mastery activities into your life. Most people with personality disorders are stuck in the rut of doing the same activities over and over again. The result is that their lives often feel boring or unfulfilling. The goal of this chapter is to help you find time in your weekly schedule for activities that give you both pleasure and a sense of accomplishment.

- In chapter 5, Challenge and Correct Self-Defeating Thoughts, you'll learn how to examine and change the way you think. People who suffer with personality disorders also struggle with many self-critical thoughts. This makes it very difficult to change anything in your life because your thoughts influence both your emotions and your behaviors. In this chapter you'll learn how that happens. Plus, you'll learn how to challenge your self-critical thoughts and develop healthier ones.

- In chapter 6, Challenge Your Negative Core Beliefs, you'll continue to examine how your thoughts affect your life. Building on the work you did in chapter 5, you'll discover your deep-seated critical beliefs and learn how they're affecting your life. Then you'll learn how to develop more balanced beliefs that will help you to create a new, healthier lifestyle. This is the most important—and most challenging—skill in this workbook.

- In chapter 7, Practice Stress-Reduction and Relaxation Techniques, you'll learn ways to calm and soothe yourself, which will help you to confront anxiety-provoking situations in a more relaxed way. This is especially important because most people with personality disorders suffer with some type of overwhelming fear or anxiety. In addition, at the end of the chapter you'll find techniques that will help you learn how to identify and describe your emotions in order to help soothe them.

- In chapter 8, Develop Problem-Solving Skills, you'll learn a technique that will help you discover new solutions to your old problems. This is helpful if you've been struggling with a frequently reoccurring problem or if you've been avoiding difficult situations that you don't know how to solve.

- In chapter 9, Develop Assertive Communication Skills, you'll learn how to communicate with others more effectively in order to protect yourself and get your needs met in an appropriate way. This is especially important if you have trouble asking for what you want or saying no, or if you're experiencing any type of relationship problem.

- In chapter 10, Learn Coping Imagery, you'll find out how to prepare for difficult, stressful situations by using visualization and coping statements. This is extremely helpful if you frequently avoid stressful situations due to fear or the belief that you won't know what to do.

- In chapter 11, Use Exposure to Confront Feared Situations and Emotions, you'll learn how to confront and cope with situations that you usually avoid, such as attending social engagements; doing things you usually put off, such as difficult tasks; or even allowing yourself to make mistakes. You'll discover how to approach these situations in a safe, systematic way by making a hierarchy for fearful experiences and then approaching the least frightening situations first, in order to build your confidence. This skill will be very helpful to most readers, but especially to those struggling with avoidant, dependent, and obsessive-compulsive personality styles. Plus, you'll learn how to confront and tolerate distressing emotional experiences, which is an especially important skill for people struggling with painful emotions, such as those who suffer with borderline personality disorder.

And finally, Part III of this workbook, Post-Treatment Care, will give you tips about what to do after you've learned and practiced all the skills you'll learn here.

- In chapter 12, Maintain Your Progress and Prevent Setbacks, you'll learn skills that will help you to maintain the progress you've made and will prevent your bad habits from returning.

IN CONCLUSION

There's no denying that changing habits is very hard, especially when you're trying to change long-standing ones like the way you think, the way you do things, the way you experience your emotions, and the way you interact with other people. But it's not impossible. Just as you'd get used to speaking a foreign language if you practiced long enough, you'll also get used to thinking, doing, feeling, and interacting with others in a new way. It just takes time and commitment.

However, that being said, it also deserves to be noted that sometimes you might need the assistance of a mental health care professional, like a psychologist or psychiatrist, to help you change those habits. You might also need the help of a professional if you're struggling with an additional psychological problem, such as depression, post-traumatic stress disorder, bipolar disorder, panic attacks, or another mental health issue. For further help in determining whether you're struggling with a problem like these, and to learn what to do about it, you might consult a book like *Getting Help: The Complete and Authoritative Guide to Self-Assessment and Treatment of Mental Health Problems*, which is also published by New Harbinger Publications.

Yes, there's no denying that it will take some hard work to change the habits associated with your personality disorder, but if you dedicate yourself to it and persevere, I have no doubt that you'll succeed.

PART I

Understanding Personality Disorders

CHAPTER 1

What Are Personality Disorders?

Many people struggle with problems that are not as easy to diagnose or treat as other mental health issues, such as phobias and panic disorder. These other difficult problems begin early in life, they influence people's behaviors, they interfere with relationships and careers, and they alter the way people think about themselves and the world. Due to the fact that these complex problems cause great distress and affect nearly every aspect of a person's life, they are officially referred to as *personality disorders*.[1]

In general, personality disorders are characterized by rigid, inflexible patterns of thinking and behaving that begin as early as childhood or adolescence and cause continual distress throughout many areas of a person's life. For example, some people with personality disorders have an excessive need to complete projects in a lengthy, step-by-step fashion that interferes with the completion of their work. Others are extremely afraid of being judged or criticized, so they frequently avoid social situations. And some people focus on pleasing others more than themselves, and as a result, they rarely get any of their own needs met.

It's estimated that almost 15 percent of all adults in the United States, or almost 31 million people, struggle with personality disorders,[2] and these types of long-term problems are often the cause of general unhappiness and disability in a person's life.[3] According to the American Psychiatric Association's *Diagnostic and Statistical Manual of Mental Disorders* (*DSM*), there are eleven personality disorders that are common to many people. These are as follows: antisocial, avoidant, borderline, dependent, histrionic, narcissistic, obsessive-compulsive, paranoid, schizoid, schizotypal, and personality disorder not otherwise specified (NOS).[1] (These are all defined later, in chapter 2.)

Many people struggle with these problems over the course of their entire lives. They recognize that their lives are often difficult, but few of them ever seek help for their problems. In fact, it is likely that few people know there is such a problem called a personality disorder. When people with these problems do seek help, it's usually for the treatment of some other problem, like depression or anxiety, while other people look for help at the urging of their family members and friends. Whatever your reason might be, whether you've picked up this book for yourself or a loved one, you've probably been suffering with some very difficult problems for a long time and haven't known where or how to get the right help. This book will teach you the skills that will loosen the grip of the personality disorder on your life. It will show you new ways to think about yourself and the world and will demonstrate new, more effective ways to meet your goals and interact with others in a more satisfying way.

Before you begin using this workbook, it's important that you first identify what type of personality disorder you're struggling with. As you'll learn later, it's possible that you may be struggling with more than one personality disorder. Or you might even be struggling with a personality disorder and another psychological problem, such as depression or anxiety. As with all health issues, it's important to identify the specific nature of your problem so that you can find the most effective treatment. The diagnostic exercise below will help you identify the type of personality style you're struggling with; however, if you suspect that you are also struggling with another mental health problem such as depression, bipolar disorder, generalized anxiety disorder, panic disorder, or any other mental health issue, you should also seek help from your medical professional or from a mental health professional, such as a psychiatrist or psychologist.

IDENTIFY YOUR PROBLEMS

In order to help you recognize the personality disorder(s) you're struggling with (or in order to confirm a diagnosis that you've already been given), read the following eleven stories. Each one describes a person who's struggling with a different personality disorder. At the end of each story, you'll learn which disorder the person has. Pay attention to the symptoms of each disorder and to the general nature of the problem. See if you recognize similar problems in your own life. If you do, record those similarities in the space provided.

Anthony

People who knew Anthony said that he was always getting into trouble ever since he was a teenager; sometimes it was serious trouble that involved him getting arrested and going to jail. In general, Anthony was both impulsive and very aggressive, which often led him to fights and putting other people's lives in danger. For example, he once was arrested for running someone off the road, and another time he attacked a man in order to steal his wallet.

In addition to being aggressive, Anthony frequently lied to people to get what he wanted. He regularly deceived others to get money from them. He regularly lied to his friends and his boss about where he was and what he was doing. Sometimes he even created fake names for himself in order to cheat people. But in spite of his efforts, Anthony was often caught because he failed to think through the outcome of his schemes. Needless to say, he could barely keep a steady job. He was constantly getting fired for lying to his bosses, stealing from his coworkers, and not coming to work when he was supposed to.

Unfortunately, Anthony didn't care much about anyone but himself. He said that the people he lied to and stole from "deserved to be taken advantage of," especially since he thought that he was smarter and more deserving than they were. Anthony had very few close relationships, and the few he did have were with people he got into trouble with. Most of the other people in his life, like his parents and ex-girlfriend, couldn't tolerate his behavior, so they stopped communicating with him.

Eventually, Anthony was arrested for stealing again, and while in prison he was assessed by a psychiatrist who diagnosed him with antisocial personality disorder.

Do you struggle with problems similar to Anthony's? What are they?

_____

_____

_____

_____

_____

_____

Ava

Being around other people made Ava feel very nervous and self-conscious. As a result, she frequently avoided social situations and group projects where she knew that she would have to interact with others. People who knew Ava described her as "very shy," and many of them thought that she didn't care about forming relationships or dating.

However, the truth was that Ava did want to form friendships and romantic relationships, but she was very afraid of being criticized and rejected. Ava thought that she wasn't as smart, as successful, or as good-looking as other people, and she often worried that others would judge her for her shortcomings or the things that she did wrong. So rather than face the possibility of humiliation or abandonment, Ava tried to minimize her contacts with people. For example, whenever colleagues from work asked her to join them at a social gathering, Ava declined, despite the fact that she really wanted to go. Her colleagues never understood why she'd refused to join them, but Ava regularly said no to any activity that might lead to her possible embarrassment.

Ava could develop a friendship with another person only after she'd been completely reassured that the person truly liked her. For example, her friend Jennifer had invited Ava to social events more than two dozen times before Ava finally accepted an invitation, and she said yes only after she felt 100 percent confident that Jennifer would not criticize her in any way. However, even after they'd been friends for some time, Ava still felt insecure because she continually compared herself to Jennifer. Ava thought that she was neither as smart nor as pretty as Jennifer, so rather than risk the possibility of being humiliated or criticized by her friend, she often agreed with Jennifer even when she didn't want to.

Luckily, one day Jennifer finally convinced Ava to seek help for her difficulties. When she saw a therapist, Ava was told that she was struggling with avoidant personality disorder.

Do you struggle with problems similar to Ava's? What are they?

_____

_____

_____

_____

_____

_____

_____

Britney

People who knew Britney were often worried about her because Britney engaged in behaviors that were harmful and even self-destructive. She frequently cut herself on purpose, acted in ways that were impulsive and dangerous (like drinking too much or having unsafe sex), and twice she'd tried to kill herself by swallowing too many pills.

Part of Britney's problem was that her mood often fluctuated. Plus, she frequently felt as though she was "empty" or "hollow" inside, in addition to feeling anxious, sad, scared, and angry most of the time. She often found that her emotions were hard to control or even cope with, especially her anger. As a result, she lashed out at others or got into arguments and fights. The stress of her intense emotions also led Britney to occasional experiences when she felt as though she was no longer connected to her body, and to occurrences when she "blacked out" or "floated away." At other times, she became excessively suspicious of other people and their motives.

Many people had tried to befriend Britney, but each new relationship had followed a similar devastating pattern. At the start of a new friendship, Britney wanted to spend all of her time with her new friend, and she often said that the person was the "best friend she'd ever had." But as soon as the new friend did something that upset Britney, her emotions drastically changed. She suddenly became angry, accused the person of betraying her, and stated that the person was the "worst friend she'd ever had." Or if Britney became afraid that she was about to be abandoned, she frantically created a situation to try to prevent that from happening. For example, she might claim to be terribly sick and ask the person to take care of her, or she might even threaten to kill herself if the person ever left her.

Britney's relationships were made even more difficult by the fact that she suffered with an unstable sense of who she was. She also frequently changed her thoughts, opinions, and goals in an attempt to redefine herself, but this often led to confusion for herself and others.

After being hospitalized for cutting herself, Britney was referred to a psychiatrist who diagnosed her with borderline personality disorder.

Do you struggle with problems similar to Britney's? What are they?

_____

_____

_____

_____

_____

_____

_____

Dwight

To his friends and coworkers, Dwight appeared unable to take care himself without asking someone else for help or advice. He consistently relied on others to tell him what to do and to show him how to do it. For example, Dwight couldn't decide what to eat for lunch without calling his girlfriend because he was afraid that he might eat "the wrong thing." Also, he frequently sought the help of coworkers on projects that he was supposed to be doing alone because he was afraid that he might "mess them up."

Dwight truly didn't think he was capable of caring for himself or making correct decisions. He had very low self-esteem and no self-confidence. He was also very afraid of offending people because he believed that if he did, he would lose their support and eventually be abandoned by them. Abandonment was the worst fate that Dwight could imagine, because he didn't think that he had the skills and the knowledge to take care of himself. As a result, he consistently tried to please others and to maintain his relationships, no matter what the cost was to himself. For example, he didn't disagree with others even when he knew they were wrong. And he was willing to tolerate unsatisfying relationships in order to ensure that he wouldn't be left alone. In fact, as soon as one friendship or romantic relationship ended, Dwight quickly jumped into a new one to take its place.

In order to make people like him and to reduce the chance of being abandoned, Dwight was also very willing to sacrifice his own needs for the needs of others. For example, he frequently gave up his lunch break to help his colleagues, and he often rearranged his weekend plans to help his friends.

After a long string of failed romances, Dwight's sister finally convinced him to seek help from a counselor, who diagnosed him with dependent personality disorder.

Do you struggle with problems similar to Dwight's? What are they?

_____

_____

_____

_____

_____

_____

Hillary

Hillary always wanted to be the center of attention, and whenever other people were around, she liked to show off. She frequently behaved in very dramatic and colorful ways, as if she were an actress on stage. Some people found her entertaining, but others weren't sure of what to make of her, especially when they noticed that Hillary's emotions shifted quickly and often seemed exaggerated.

Hillary also had a strong need to impress people. She often tried to amaze others with her knowledge of current events, but despite her strong opinions, her true knowledge of these issues was often limited. So whenever people would ask her additional questions about what she thought, she would change the subject to distract them. At other times, she simply changed her opinions and behaviors to match those of people she admired, like her friends, so that she could appear to be as smart and impressive as they were.

When her usual methods of getting attention didn't work, Hillary often flirted or acted seductively. She even flirted with strangers and treated people she had just met as if they were her lifelong friends. At other times, she resorted to wearing provocative clothing to draw attention to the way she looked. To some people this behavior might have seemed inappropriate, but to Hillary being flirtatious was a highly successful way to get noticed.

Hillary loved getting attention and being admired. However, when she didn't get what she wanted, she often became frustrated. Sometimes she would make a scene to get others to notice her. At other times, she would simply leave the event when she wasn't the center of attention.

Eventually, Hillary became frustrated by her lack of close, genuine friendships and she sought the help of a psychologist, who diagnosed her with histrionic personality disorder.

Do you struggle with problems similar to Hillary's? What are they?

_____

_____

_____

_____

_____

_____

Nathan

Nathan thought very highly of himself. Generally, he thought that he was smarter, better-looking, and more accomplished than other people; as a result, he also thought that he deserved more praise and admiration than they did. Nathan frequently bragged about his special attributes, but very rarely did he receive the praise he thought he deserved. This surprised him, but he assumed that others were just jealous of him, just as he was often jealous of others who had succeeded when he had not.

Nathan often fantasized about his future successes. He daydreamed that someone of great status would recognize his accomplishments and finally award him the recognition and power he deserved. In fact, Nathan believed that only people of great wealth, fame, or power could truly understand him, so he chose to associate with only the most successful and smartest people he could find. In general, Nathan had little empathy for those who were "less" than he, and he thought his accomplishments entitled him to take advantage of them for his own purposes. For example, in busy stores, he often went directly to the front of the line despite how many people were waiting. While at work, he often gave orders to his coworkers, even to those who were his equals or superiors.

Needless to say, Nathan's need for admiration and his lack of empathy greatly interfered with his relationships. At the urging of his general practitioner, Nathan sought help from the best therapist he could find to help him understand why other people were so unfriendly toward him. After a few weeks of therapy, his therapist diagnosed him with narcissistic personality disorder.

Do you struggle with problems similar to Nathan's? What are they?

_____

_____

_____

_____

_____

_____

Olivia

Olivia was a perfectionist who was very concerned with following rules, making lists, and staying on schedule. Everything she did at home and at work had to be completed according to her own set of very high standards. This meant that Olivia's tasks were completed very slowly—and sometimes not completed at all—since she frequently rechecked all of the details. This need for perfection greatly upset both her family and her boss because they were forced to wait for her to complete her tasks. However, when they offered to help her, Olivia declined.

Olivia found it very difficult to delegate tasks to others because she worried that they would not follow her procedures and the task would not be completed the way she wanted it to be. Some called her stubborn or suggested other ways of doing things, but Olivia strongly resisted any changes, new ideas, and compromises. Instead, to complete her projects, she worked very long hours. Some described her as a workaholic because she worked late into the evenings and throughout most weekends. Olivia rarely took time off, and when she did, she usually brought unfinished work with her. Not surprisingly, even her vacations were highly organized, structured, and active. Instead of relaxing during her time off, she preferred vacations that focused on mastering very difficult tasks, like scuba diving or mountain climbing.

Despite the fact that Olivia did not consider herself to be a religious person, she still had very rigid moral standards and rules for herself and others. For example, Olivia expected that everyone in her housing development should strictly abide by all of the rules, as she did, and she made frequent complaints about those who didn't. Similarly, her children had to do their homework perfectly; otherwise, she made them do it over again.

Throughout the years, Olivia also engaged in other behaviors that caused her family to worry about her. First, there was her habit of collecting old magazines, things she found on the street, and broken items that her family had wanted to throw away. Over the years, Olivia had filled entire rooms with such things because she said she might need them some day. Second, she forced her family to live on a very restricted, small budget and saved the rest of the money for future emergencies, despite the fact that her family sometimes had to live without basic necessities, like toilet paper.

Eventually, Olivia's family convinced her to seek help. After being evaluated by her social worker, Olivia was diagnosed with obsessive-compulsive personality disorder.

Do you struggle with problems similar to Olivia's? What are they?

_____

_____

_____

_____

_____

_____

_____

Patrick

Patrick was always worrying about other people's intentions. He frequently thought that someone was trying to hurt him, take advantage of him, or deceive him in some way. But very seldom could he or anyone else find any evidence that this was happening. Instead, Patrick merely suspected that it was happening, and as a result, it was very hard for him to trust people and develop close relationships.

Patrick even doubted the loyalty of his family, longtime friends, and coworkers he had known for years. His suspicious beliefs prevented him from trusting anyone, and he was constantly searching for proof of his suspicions, no matter how small that proof might be. For example, a friend of his at work had once said that he liked another coworker whom Patrick didn't care for. But instead of letting the comment go, Patrick interpreted this harmless remark as meaning that his friend could no longer be trusted, and Patrick stopped speaking to him.

Behaviors like this made it very difficult to get to know Patrick. In addition, he rarely confided in other people or shared any details of his life with anyone. If someone were to ask him a question, Patrick would refuse to answer because he worried that the person would use that information against him.

He was so worried about getting hurt that he often misinterpreted harmless jokes and remarks, which he'd mistakenly thought were made at his expense. For example, whenever a coworker offered help with a task or project, Patrick thought this meant that the person was trying to get close to him so that he or she could uncover his mistakes and use them against him.

Also, Patrick was quick to get angry, and he held on to grudges. Rarely did Patrick forgive anyone who had done something that he perceived as a threat.

Occasionally, Patrick dated, but his jealousy and desire to control the other person eventually drove the person away. In fact, he was so jealous of one girlfriend that he kept a journal of her actions in an effort to catch her in a lie.

After experiencing many difficulties like the ones described, Patrick eventually sought help from his employees' assistance program, and a counselor diagnosed him with paranoid personality disorder.

Do you struggle with problems similar to Patrick's? What are they?

_____

_____

_____

_____

_____

_____

Scarlett

People who knew Scarlett often described her as a loner because she wasn't interested in forming friendships or romantic relationships. However, Scarlett was neither angry nor jealous of other people; she just preferred to be by herself. She hardly ever visited her parents and brother, she very rarely dated, and her job as a computer technician required little interaction with anyone but her supervisor. In general, Scarlett preferred to be alone, and she didn't feel the need to seek companionship. To relax, she preferred solitary pleasurable activities, like reading and puzzles, and she did little else with her free time since her interests were so limited.

People who knew Scarlett, such as her supervisor and parents, had a very hard time figuring her out. In addition to not forming close relationships, Scarlett appeared uninterested in what other people thought of her. Regardless of whether her supervisor praised or criticized her, Scarlett remained unaffected and indifferent. In fact, people often said that it was difficult to tell what she was thinking because she rarely displayed any emotions. Sometimes people would tell her to smile or cheer up, but the truth was, she didn't think she had to. Scarlett seldom expressed her emotions in a way that other people could see and recognize.

Her parents wondered if she would ever marry, since she seldom dated. However, Scarlett didn't seem to feel the need for close companionship or a sexual relationship the way other people do. Occasionally, her parents or someone at work would arrange a blind date for her, but it never worked out. Sometimes Scarlett worried about her future and the possibility of being alone, but usually she kept her thoughts and feelings to herself rather than talk to someone about them.

However, at the urging of her mother, Scarlett agreed to seek help from a psychologist, who diagnosed her with schizoid personality disorder.

Do you struggle with problems similar to Scarlett's? What are they?

_____

_____

_____

_____

_____

_____

_____

Scott

Scott found it very difficult to connect with people, and he frequently felt odd and out of place in social situations. Often, he didn't know what to do or say around others, and he regularly found himself being stared at as he awkwardly tried to fit in with one or another social group. For example, Scott sometimes laughed at stories that no one else found funny, and he often remained quiet while everyone else discussed an exciting topic. Even Scott's style of dress regularly made him feel out of place—his wide-brimmed cowboy hat and purple pants often drew stares and rude remarks from people on the street.

Many of Scott's interests and beliefs also got strange reactions when he shared them with others. For example, Scott was very interested in paranormal experiences, and he often believed that his thoughts could control or affect other people's actions. He also experienced sensing or seeing things that others could not, like the strange shadows he occasionally saw dancing in the trees. However, sometimes odd things happened that even Scott wasn't sure about, like the night he thought the television newscaster had been speaking directly to him.

In addition to experiences like this, Scott also found it difficult to communicate with most people. Sometimes his own thoughts were too unclear; at other times, people told him he was being too vague or that he was taking too long to make his point.

Regardless of how often Scott tried to connect with others, he generally felt anxious and was unable to relax in social situations, even after getting to know people better. The truth was that Scott was suspicious of many people, partly due to the strange stares and comments he frequently received from strangers, but also partly due to the fact that he found it hard to trust anyone. As a result, he didn't have many close friends. His closest relationship was with his brother, but he seldom spoke to his brother.

Thankfully, however, his brother convinced Scott that he should see a therapist for help with his social awkwardness. After a few sessions, Scott's therapist diagnosed him with schizotypal personality disorder.

Do you struggle with problems similar to Scott's? What are they?

_____

_____

_____

_____

_____

_____

_____

Vivian

Vivian also struggled with repetitive, long-term problems that interfered with her relationships, her job, and her life in general. In fact, she struggled with many of the same problems described in previous examples, but none of the previous examples accurately describe Vivian's own difficulties. For example, like Britney, Vivian was afraid of being abandoned, but she didn't engage in self-destructive behaviors and her mood didn't fluctuate as Britney's did. Like Nathan, Vivian thought very highly of herself and that she was smarter than most people, but she didn't always need to be admired as Nathan did, and neither did she feel entitled to take advantage of others. And like Patrick, Vivian often worried about other people's intentions and whether they could be trusted. But unlike Patrick, Vivian was able to maintain some close relationships.

In general, Vivian's problems were similar to all of the other examples cited, but no one example fully describes her own unique difficulties. In fact, Vivian had one problem that was very different: she often procrastinated and frequently refused to do what was asked of her. For example, she often felt unappreciated by her boss, but rather than talk to him about how she felt, she sometimes refused to do her work and then blamed her coworkers when it wasn't completed on time.

After being reprimanded by her boss, Vivian sought the help of a therapist, who diagnosed her with a personality disorder, but since Vivian's symptoms didn't fit the criteria for any specific disorder, the therapist labeled her problem personality disorder not otherwise specified (NOS).

Do you struggle with problems similar to Vivian's? What are they?

_____

_____

_____

_____

_____

_____

_____

_____

IN CONCLUSION

Now that you've finished reading each of the descriptions, go back and review the comments you made after each of them. Is there one particular example whose problem is similar to yours? Or were there several examples that were similar to yours? What personality disorders were those individuals struggling with? Note them for the next chapter. When you're ready, continue by reading chapter 2, where you'll learn more information.

CHAPTER 2

The Eleven Personality Disorders

Now that you've read the descriptions of the eleven personality disorders in chapter 1, hopefully you were able to identify the personality disorder you're struggling with. Or maybe you recognized that you're struggling with more than one disorder or with the characteristics of a few different disorders. If that is the case, now would be a good time to seek the opinion of a mental health care professional who can confirm or correct your diagnosis, since only a trained professional, such as a psychologist or psychiatrist, can accurately diagnosis your problem.

However, assuming that you've already sought the help of a professional or that you are currently working with one, now you're ready to read more detailed information about each of the personality disorders. You can choose to read all of the descriptions or just the ones you're struggling with. But before you begin reading about your specific problem, it's important to note that there are a few characteristics that apply to all personality disorders:[1]

1. The traits of a personality disorder often begin as early as childhood or adolescence, but definitely by early adulthood.

2. The traits affect your thoughts, emotions, behaviors, impulses, and relationships.

3. The traits of all personality disorders are inflexible and difficult to change.

4. Personality disorders affect many areas of your life, such as work, school, family life, and friendships, and they cause great distress.

5. The traits and habits of a personality disorder are very different from the traits and habits that are expected within your culture. For example, if your culture encourages submissive behavior, this trait should not be considered a symptom of dependent personality disorder.

6. If your problems are caused by a medical problem, a different mental health problem (such as depression), or by drug or alcohol addiction, a personality disorder would not be the correct diagnosis.

Note: If you don't meet these six criteria, you probably don't have a fully developed personality disorder. You might have only some of the traits of one. However, the skills in this workbook will still be extremely helpful to you.

Now continue reading about the specific personality disorders you identified as problems. Do your best to read these descriptions with an open, honest, and accepting state of mind. Remember, no one wants to struggle with any of these problems, but it's important to know what you're up against. When you're done, turn to the end of this chapter and continue reading about the different causes of personality disorders.

ANTISOCIAL PERSONALITY DISORDER

People who have *antisocial personality disorder* manipulate and abuse others for their own purposes and show little or no consideration for the needs and safety of others.[1]

If you have this type of personality disorder, you can often be violent, impatient, self-centered, and easily agitated. Most likely, you also show little regret when you hurt others and you pay little attention to rules and the law, which often puts you at risk of being arrested. A person with an antisocial personality frequently thinks that other people aren't as smart as he or she is, and therefore they deserve to be manipulated. For these reasons, a person with this problem seldom has close friends or romantic relationships.

According to the American Psychiatric Association, an official diagnosis of antisocial personality disorder would be made if you met several criteria.[1] First, for this diagnosis to be made, you must be at least eighteen years old, and you must have a history of harming, disrespecting, or violating the rights of others since you were fifteen years old; in addition, you must have engaged in similar rebellious behaviors earlier in your life. Second, at least three of the following types of harmful behavior should be observed:

1. You repeatedly engage in behaviors that break the law and potentially lead to getting arrested.

2. You lie or manipulate others for your own pleasure or personal gain.

3. Your behavior is often impulsive or you repeatedly fail to plan ahead.

4. Your behavior could be described as "violent" or "bad-tempered," based on the fact that you're regularly involved in fights or attacks on others.

5. Your behaviors put your own life or the lives of others in danger.

6. You regularly fail to take responsibility for your work or your financial obligations.

7. You don't feel guilt or regret for harming or taking advantage of others.

Obviously, the most frequently observed problem related to this disorder is breaking the law. In surveys of prison populations, the rate of antisocial personality disorder has been as high as 60 percent for both men[4] and women.[5]

People with antisocial personalities are also at a higher risk of dying from unnatural causes. In one long-term study, people with this type of personality were almost four times as likely to die when compared with other people.[6] Among the many reasons for this likelihood are an increased risk for suicide,[7] an increased risk for accidents,[8] and an increased risk of experiencing a violent death.[9]

Many people with antisocial personalities also struggle with phobias, post-traumatic stress disorder, panic disorder, generalized anxiety disorder, depression, bipolar disorder,[10] alcohol and drug problems,[11] and gambling addictions.[12]

In a large study of adults in the United States, it was estimated that almost 4 percent of that population, or almost 8 million people, had antisocial personalities, with men being affected more often than women.[2]

AVOIDANT PERSONALITY DISORDER

People who have *avoidant personality disorders* are very sensitive to criticism and judgment from others, so they tend to stay away from social interactions.[1]

If you're struggling with this problem, you probably want to have relationships with other people, but most likely, you're also very critical of your own social skills and self-worth. You might think that you're defective or somehow substandard in comparison to others, and so you avoid social and work situations in which you might be evaluated, criticized, humiliated, or rejected. This avoidance probably prevents you from meeting or interacting with others unless you can be sure that they will like you. As a result, others might describe you as shy, a loner, or introverted.

According to the American Psychiatric Association, an official diagnosis of avoidant personality disorder would be made if you experienced at least four of the following symptoms that began by early adulthood and were observable in several different situations:[1]

1. You avoid work activities that might include significant social interactions due to your fear of being criticized, shamed, or rejected.

2. You proceed cautiously in romantic and other close relationships due to a fear of being humiliated or ridiculed.

3. You frequently think about being judged, evaluated, or rejected in social situations.

4. You're hesitant to form new relationships unless you're sure that you'll be liked.

5. You proceed cautiously in new relationships and social situations because you feel defective or incompetent.

6. You think that you lack social skills, are inferior to others, or are unattractive in some way.

7. You're cautious about trying new activities or taking personal risks because you might be embarrassed or humiliated.

In addition to having few close relationships, people who have avoidant personalities also struggle with problems at work, depression, anxiety, and other personality disorders.[1]

It's estimated that approximately 1 percent of the general population has avoidant personality disorder.[1]

BORDERLINE PERSONALITY DISORDER

People who have *borderline personality disorder* suffer frequent, uncontrollable, and painful mood swings.[1] They also experience great difficulty forming and maintaining relationships, they have problems controlling their own impulsive and reckless behaviors, and they experience fluctuating ideas about who they are.[1]

If you struggle with this disorder, you frequently experience rapid and unpredictable changes in your thoughts, moods, behaviors, relationships, and beliefs.[13] Very often, these rapid changes are caused by recurring fears of being criticized or abandoned by other people, or by the actions of other people that feel like criticism, such as disagreements or changes in plans. In response to these types of situations, you probably experience sudden feelings of sadness, nervousness, or anger. You might also engage in some type of impulsive self-harming behavior, such as self-mutilation, unsafe sexual activity, or suicidal acts.[14]

According to the American Psychiatric Association, an official diagnosis of borderline personality disorder would be made if you experienced at least five of the following symptoms that began by early adulthood and were observable in several different situations:[1]

1. You experience unstable emotions that change impulsively and are often painful.

2. You experience intense anger that is difficult to control and often arises at times that seem unexpected to others.

3. You experience frequent feelings of worthlessness or emptiness.

4. Your relationships are frequently unstable and intense, and you often fluctuate between first praising others and then quickly criticizing them.

5. You behave in agitated or frantic ways to avoid being abandoned by others.

6. You behave in ways that are both impulsive and potentially damaging to yourself, such as engaging in unsafe sex, spending excessive amounts of money, or using excessive amounts of alcohol.

7. You regularly engage in behaviors related to suicide, such as making threats or attempts, or you engage in self-mutilating behaviors, such as cutting.

8. You have a very uncertain or unstable sense of self-identity; that is, you're not sure "who you are."

9. During periods of stress you either have powerful thoughts that someone is trying to harm you or you feel strangely distant or disconnected from your body or your thoughts—a condition that is called *dissociation*.

Of all the problems related to borderline personality, the most severe is suicide. It's estimated that as many as 75 percent of the people with this problem will attempt to kill themselves at some point,[15] and as many as 10 percent eventually will take their own lives.[16] In addition, many people with borderline personality disorder suffer with depression, post-traumatic stress disorder, eating disorders, phobias, panic disorder, and drug and alcohol problems.[17] Males suffering from borderline personality disorder seem to be more likely to develop drug or alcohol problems than female sufferers. But female sufferers appear to be more likely to develop bulimia, anorexia, and other eating disorders.[18] People with borderline personality disorder also frequently suffer with chronic medical conditions such as fibromyalgia, chronic fatigue syndrome, obesity, diabetes, hypertension, arthritis, and back pain.[19]

Studies have estimated that as much as 5 percent of the general population is affected by borderline personality disorder.[3] Many studies report that almost 75 percent of the people diagnosed with this problem are women.[20] However, this striking outcome isn't always found,[18] and a few researchers have uncovered evidence that some mental health professionals diagnose women with borderline personality disorder more frequently than men, even when both sexes have the same symptoms.[21]

DEPENDENT PERSONALITY DISORDER

People with *dependent personality disorder* are unable to make decisions without the constant assistance and approval of others, so they constantly rely on others to take care of them and to make decisions for them.[1]

If you have this problem, you often find it difficult to make even ordinary, everyday decisions without the help of others, such as what clothes to wear, what to eat, and where to go. Most likely, you don't think that you're good enough or smart enough to make those decisions for yourself. In addition, you're probably afraid that if you do something wrong, you'll be abandoned by others. As a result, you're constantly trying to please others by seeking approval, volunteering for unpleasant chores, and not disagreeing.

According to the American Psychiatric Association, an official diagnosis of dependent personality disorder would be made if you experienced at least five of the following problems that began by early adulthood and were observable in several different situations:[1]

1. You frequently struggle with making regular, everyday decisions if you don't receive an excessive amount of help and reassurance from other people.

2. You need other people to take on the responsibility of caring for many of the major areas of your life, such as your career, friendships, and finances.

3. You avoid disagreeing with other people because you're afraid that they will no longer like you or help you in the future.

4. You avoid taking on projects or doing things on your own due to a lack of confidence in your own ability to make decisions.

5. You go to great lengths to make other people like you and help you, which includes volunteering to do things that are unpleasant or that you really don't want to do.

6. You feel uncomfortable or vulnerable when you're alone because you don't think that you can take care of yourself.

7. You quickly become involved in a new relationship with another person to help you soon after a previous relationship has ended.

8. You're often frightened by thoughts about having to care for yourself.

Despite their best efforts to please others, many people with dependent personality disorder do not have close, satisfying relationships in which their own needs are met.[22] People with this type of personality are also in danger of experiencing problems such as depression, bipolar disorder, panic disorder, generalized anxiety disorder, bulimia, and social phobia.[10] There's also an increased risk of suicide among people with dependent personalities.[23] Other studies have found relatively strong relationships between dependent personality and alcohol and drug problems, especially for men.[11]

It's estimated that approximately 1 percent of the general adult population has a dependent personality,[24] with women developing the problem more often than men.[2]

HISTRIONIC PERSONALITY DISORDER

People who have *histrionic personality disorders* frequently want to be the center of attention and often act in very dramatic ways in order to be noticed.[1]

If you have this type of personality disorder, you probably spend a lot of time thinking of ways to get attention and make people like you. For example, you might dress or act seductively to make people look at you, you might act in a grandiose way as if you were performing on stage, or you might treat new acquaintances as if they were the most important people you've ever met. Additionally, you most likely experience emotions that change quickly and appear exaggerated to others. Plus, if someone doesn't return the feelings you have for him or her or pay sufficient attention to what you're doing, you probably react very dramatically, by acting extremely hurt, making a scene, or leaving.

According to the American Psychiatric Association, an official diagnosis of histrionic personality disorder would be made if you experienced at least five of the following symptoms that began by early adulthood and were observable in several different situations:[1]

1. You want to be the center of attention in most situations, and you feel upset, uncomfortable, or angry when you're not.

2. You behave in ways that are sexually seductive or attention grabbing in order to make other people notice you.

3. You regularly use your physical appearance to make people notice you.

4. Your emotions change rather quickly and might appear thin or insincere to others.

5. Your behaviors appear dramatic or showy, as if you're acting on stage, or your emotions are more intense than what is necessary.

6. You often voice strong opinions about particular subjects without having many facts to support your opinions.

7. You treat people as if you know them better than you really do, such as treating new acquaintances as if they were your best friends.

8. You easily change your opinions and feelings in order to please others, especially people you respect or admire.

People with histrionic personality disorder also frequently struggle with strained relationships, suicidal behaviors, depression, and other personality disorders.[1]

It's estimated that approximately 3 percent of the general population struggles with histrionic personality disorder.[1]

NARCISSISTIC PERSONALITY DISORDER

People who have *narcissistic personality disorder* believe that they have many exceptional characteristics and are entitled to the admiration of others; plus, they often lack sympathy and compassion for others.[1]

If you have a narcissistic personality, you're often preoccupied with your own success, intelligence, and attractiveness. It's very important to you that others see you as influential, talented, beautiful, intelligent, and persuasive. You might also think that you're entitled to special attention from others. Or you might believe that you can be truly understood only by others like you, so you associate only with people of high status. People with narcissistic personalities often consider others to be of lesser worth than they are, so they often criticize others for their faults, act enviously of others' successes, or take advantage of others to get their own needs met.

In general, there appear to be two different types of people with narcissistic personality disorder: those who are outgoing in social situations and those who are not.[25] If you're outgoing, you like to show off and be the focus of attention. You probably put a lot of time into preparing the way you look and you expect others to pay you compliments, and if they don't, you become offended or angry.[26] If you're not outgoing, you like to keep to yourself and you probably get upset when you're criticized, so you put great effort into protecting yourself from disapproval.

According to the American Psychiatric Association, an official diagnosis of narcissistic personality disorder would be made if you experienced at least five of the following symptoms that began by early adulthood and were observable in several different situations:[1]

1. You have a superior opinion of yourself, your abilities, and your achievements, even though you sometimes overestimate these qualities.

2. You often fantasize about your own success, power, intelligence, or attractiveness—perhaps comparing yourself to other successful or famous people—and you often expect to be recognized or praised for your special traits.

3. You think that you're exceptional or superior in some way; therefore, you can be truly understood only by other superior people and you should associate only with them.

4. You need frequent admiration and compliments from others.

5. You expect to be treated in a special way based upon your exceptional characteristics.

6. You believe that your needs are more important than the needs of others, so you take advantage of others for your own benefit.

7. You generally don't think about or care about other people's feelings or needs.

8. You're frequently jealous of other people, especially their successes, or you frequently think that other people are jealous of you.

9. Other people describe your behavior or attitude as arrogant, snobbish, or conceited.

Due to the characteristics of this type of problem, it's often very hard for someone with a narcissistic personality to maintain romantic relationships.[27] Many people with narcissistic personality problems also suffer with bipolar disorder,[28] depression,[1] and anxiety problems.[29] There's also a danger of developing problems with substance abuse,[30] gambling addiction,[31] and eating disorders.[32] However, the greatest threat for people with narcissistic personalities is the possibility of suicide.[33] It has been observed that suicide attempts can arise very quickly and without warning in people with this problem,[33] possibly resulting from a sudden injury to the person's self-esteem.[34]

It's estimated that less than 1 percent of the general population has narcissistic personality disorder,[3] with men diagnosed with the problem more often than women.[35]

OBSESSIVE-COMPULSIVE PERSONALITY DISORDER

People who have *obsessive-compulsive personality disorder* are very concerned with maintaining order and control, achieving perfection, and following rules.[1]

If you struggle with this problem, it's probably very difficult for you to complete tasks because you can't complete them perfectly. People with obsessive-compulsive personality disorder might be described as very conscientious students or workers, but they often have trouble getting projects finished on time because they must follow their own step-by-step procedures or constantly revise whatever they're working on. You also might find it very difficult to delegate work to others unless you can control the quality of what they do.

Most likely, this need for perfection interferes with your social activities and relationships, since you put them on hold until you complete unfinished projects. You also might be equally rigid when it comes to following moral principles and the rules of law. People with this type of personality believe that others should behave as they do, and they get very upset or angry when others don't follow the rules.

In severe cases of obsessive-compulsive personality disorder, you might collect and hide things because you fear that you might need them in the future. This is called hoarding. For example, you might collect old, valueless objects like newspapers or items you find on the street. In other cases, you might hide all of your money and live a meager lifestyle, fearing that one day you will need the money for a catastrophe.

According to the American Psychiatric Association, an official diagnosis of obsessive-compulsive personality disorder would be made if you experienced at least four of the following symptoms that began by early adulthood and were observable in several different situations:[1]

1. You're often fixated on following rules, making lists, maintaining order, or paying attention to details, which, unfortunately, often becomes more important to you than the overall activity you're working on.

2. Your desire to do something perfectly often interferes with your ability to finish a task.

3. You're often willing to neglect your family, friends, and personal life in order to spend more time at work.

4. You live your life according to a very strict set of morals, rules, and values—other than your religious or cultural principles—and you often expect others to follow the same strict standards.

5. You find it very difficult—if not impossible—to assign tasks to others or to work with others unless you can control how they do things.

6. You collect worthless objects and can't get rid of them, even if they have no personal value, because you think that you might need them in the future.

7. You maintain a very meager lifestyle that is far below what you can afford so that you can save money for future emergencies.

8. Other people would describe your behavior as inflexible or stubborn because you are unwilling to compromise on how things should be done.

People with obsessive-compulsive personalities also struggle with anxiety disorders such as generalized anxiety disorder and phobias.[1] This type of personality disorder also shares traits with another anxiety disorder with a similar name, *obsessive-compulsive disorder*, but this problem involves intrusive thoughts that a person tries to neutralize with compulsive behaviors.

It's estimated that approximately 1 percent of the general population struggles with obsessive-compulsive personality disorder.[1]

PARANOID PERSONALITY DISORDER

People who have *paranoid personality disorder* are very mistrustful of others and their motives, even when there is little or no evidence to support their suspicions.[1]

If you have this type of personality disorder, you're constantly on the lookout for being attacked, injured, or tricked by other people,[36] including friends, family, and coworkers. You might even suspect that your friends and family members are plotting to harm you.

People with this problem are always questioning the loyalty of others, and any deviation from 100 percent loyalty is interpreted as a betrayal. As a result, you probably have damaged your family relationships and have few close friends or social interactions. You also might hold grudges, get extremely jealous, react angrily when you think you've been insulted, and try to control other people's lives.[1]

According to the American Psychiatric Association, an official diagnosis of paranoid personality disorder would be made if you experienced at least four of the following symptoms that began by early adulthood and were observable in several different situations:[1]

1. You think that other people are trying to harm you or take advantage of you, even if you don't have reasonable proof to support your suspicions.

2. You often think that your friends, family, or coworkers aren't loyal and can't be trusted.

3. You find it difficult—if not impossible—to trust other people with information because you suspect that they might use that information to harm you.

4. You often suspect that people are making concealed threats or insults, even though their words and actions might appear harmless to others.

5. You find it difficult—if not impossible—to forgive others for their wrongdoings and you often feel resentment toward them.

6. If you suspect that someone is trying to insult or harm you, you become irritated or quickly fight back.

7. You often suspect that your spouse or romantic partner is betraying you, even if you don't have reasonable proof to support your suspicions.

Many people with paranoid personality disorders also suffer with other problems, such as drug and alcohol addictions,[11] depression, bipolar disorder, panic disorder, phobias, and generalized anxiety disorder.[10]

It's estimated that nearly 4 percent of the general adult population struggles with paranoid personality disorder,[2] with women reporting the problem more frequently than men.[2]

SCHIZOID PERSONALITY DISORDER

People who have *schizoid personality disorder* aren't interested in seeking social contacts or relationships, and they often prefer to be alone.[1] They also aren't concerned about receiving either approval or criticism from others and show little emotional response to other people and events.[37]

If you struggle with this problem, others might describe you as very shy, reclusive, or even unfriendly—despite what you really think and feel. You actually might like being around other people, but maybe you just don't know how to interact with them,[38] or maybe you feel extremely uncomfortable when you try to interact.[36] Either way, you probably avoid unnecessary contact with others and prefer to have a job that requires little interaction with people. Also, if you do have relationships, they're probably not very intimate.

According to the American Psychiatric Association, an official diagnosis of schizoid personality disorder would be made if you experienced at least four of the following symptoms that began by early adulthood and were observable in several different situations:[1]

1. You don't want close relationships with others, nor do you receive pleasure from having close relationships, even with members of your own family.

2. You frequently—if not always—choose to engage in activities and tasks that you can do by yourself.

3. You're not interested in having sexual relationships.

4. You find pleasure in very few pursuits or hobbies—if you have any interests at all.

5. You have few close friends or people with whom you talk freely, other than your family members.

6. You're not interested in receiving compliments from other people, nor do you care when others evaluate you negatively. Or if you are interested in these judgments, you don't allow others to see your reactions to them.

7. Your range of emotional reactions, facial gestures, or social behaviors often appears very limited to yourself and to others. Others might interpret this as you being cold or rude, but you might not experience many strong emotions or you might not know how to act in social situations.

Many people with this type of personality disorder also struggle with bipolar disorder, depression, panic disorder, generalized anxiety disorder, and social phobia,[10] as well as drug and alcohol problems.[11] Additionally, there appears to be a strong link between schizoid personality disorder and the development of problems such as schizophrenia[39] and homelessness.[40]

In a large study of adults in the United States, it was estimated that 3 percent of that population had schizoid personalities, with men and women affected equally.[2]

SCHIZOTYPAL PERSONALITY DISORDER

People who have *schizotypal personality disorders* have difficulties forming and maintaining relationships, exhibit eccentric behavior that doesn't fit in with the rest of society, and will often have unusual or suspicious thoughts.[1]

If you struggle with this type of personality, you might want close relationships but lack the necessary social skills to form them or you may feel very uncomfortable when you try to create them. As a result, you probably have few social contacts.

For some people with schizotypal personalities, the problem of creating close relationships is related to their eccentric habits. When compared with the rest of society, people with schizotypal personalities often dress or act in ways that appear unusual or unconventional. Some people with this type of personality style even claim to have special powers or psychic abilities. For example, some people believe that they can cause common events, like making someone call them just by thinking about the person, while others believe that certain events have a special meaning for them, such as "Every time the sun comes up, it's the universe's way of saying hello to me."

According to the American Psychiatric Association, an official diagnosis of schizotypal personality disorder would be made if you experienced at least five of the following symptoms that began by early adulthood and were observable in several different situations:[1]

1. You believe that certain commonplace events have a special meaning for you, even if you don't have reasonable proof or they appear unrelated to you in the opinion of others.

2. You believe that you have magical abilities or supernatural powers, such as the ability to predict events before they happen, move objects with the power of your mind, or communicate with the dead. You might also be very superstitious or even engage in certain rituals to ward off danger.

3. You have unusual experiences that involve your senses, such as hearing someone say something when no one's nearby, seeing things that aren't there, or sensing things that aren't really present, such as another person standing beside you.

4. Compared to other people in your culture or society, you think and speak in an unusual or eccentric way. For example, you might make up words or phrases, you might give extremely detailed answers to every question you're asked, or you might give vague responses that always require additional explanation.

5. You think that other people are trying to harm you or take advantage of you, even if you don't have reasonable proof to support your suspicions.

6. Your range of emotional reactions, facial gestures, or social behaviors often appears very limited to yourself or others. Others might interpret this as being cold or rude, but maybe you just don't know how to act in social situations.

7. Compared to others in your society or culture, your actions or appearance are considered out of the ordinary or eccentric by yourself or others. For example, during conversations, you might say things that make other people stop and look at you strangely, or you might dress in clothes that are drastically different in style from everyone else's.

8. You have very few close friends with whom you talk freely, other than your family members.

9. You're very nervous when you're around other people, especially people you don't know very well. In addition, you're often worried about what others are thinking about you. You may be nervous that they're trying to harm you, or perhaps you're worried because you don't fit in with them or the rest of society.

Many people with schizotypal personality disorder also struggle with anxiety and depression, as well as with brief psychotic episodes that are often caused by stress.[1]

It's estimated that schizotypal personality disorder occurs in almost 3 percent of the general population.[1]

PERSONALITY DISORDER NOT OTHERWISE SPECIFIED

People who have a personality disorder not otherwise specified (NOS) do not meet the criteria for any single type of personality disorder.

If you have personality disorder NOS, you might have several traits from one or more of the personality types described above but not meet the full requirements for that category. For example, you might struggle with making ordinary decisions without obtaining an excessive amount of help and reassurance from other people, and you frequently avoid disagreeing with others, but you don't meet any of the other requirements for a diagnosis of dependent personality disorder. Or maybe you identified symptoms from the categories of borderline, narcissistic, and histrionic personality disorders, but again, you don't meet the full requirements of any of them.

In other cases, you might be diagnosed with personality disorder NOS if you meet the full requirements of the disorders in general; that is, inflexible traits and behaviors that begin no later than early adulthood and interfere with many areas of your life, but those traits and behaviors are different than the ones described in the ten categories above. For example, some researchers have proposed the idea of recognizing passive-aggressive personality disorder.[1] A person with this type of personality resists doing his or her work or meeting a job's requirements and frequently feels resentful of others.

It's not known how many people struggle with personality disorder NOS or what types of related problems exist. However, they're probably very similar to many of the other personality problems described above.

THE CAUSES OF PERSONALITY DISORDERS

If you're like most people struggling with a personality disorder, you're probably wondering why you have these problems in the first place. The truth is there are many possible reasons.

Personality disorders are most likely caused by a combination of biological, psychological, and social factors. Some studies have shown that personality disorders have a strong chance of being passed on in families due to influential genetic traits.[41] Other studies have linked the development of various personality disorders to factors such as brain abnormalities,[42] childhood experiences of depression and anxiety,[43] parental depression,[44] parenting styles,[45] childhood temper and activity levels,[46] a history of being abused or neglected,[47] having a family member with schizophrenia,[48] poverty,[3] and nutritional deficits.[49] Certain personality traits can also be learned by watching the behaviors of parents.[50]

Unfortunately, you might never know the exact cause of your problem, but that doesn't mean you can't do anything about it. The problems associated with your personality disorder are very treatable if you're willing to dedicate some time and effort to learning new coping skills.

IN CONCLUSION

Personality disorders aren't fair to the people they affect. There's often no known cause, and there are no easy fixes to make them go away. The truth is this: you're the only person who can fix your problems, and to your credit, you've already picked up this book and started working. You've now completed the first two chapters, and hopefully you've identified your problem and have a better understanding of how it's affecting your life.

As you continue reading, remember that the name of your problem isn't what's important. What's important is that you've been struggling with a difficult problem for a very long time, and now you're looking to improve your life. Continue reading; the next chapter will help you to learn how to do this.

CHAPTER 3

Cognitive Behavioral Therapy for Personality Disorders

This chapter will explain what cognitive behavioral therapy (CBT) is and how it will help you learn new coping skills. Note that if you already know about CBT or you just want to begin learning the skills, you can feel free to skip this chapter.

EARLY TREATMENT METHODS

Prior to the 1950s, the field of psychology was dominated by the theories of Sigmund Freud and his belief that mental health problems were caused by people's unconscious conflicts and their attempts to repress or avoid those conflicts. For example, imagine that a woman finds out that her husband is having an affair. She feels very angry and resentful, and secretly she wants to divorce him, but her religious values won't allow her to do that. As a result, her thoughts and feelings get pushed down out of her awareness and become unconscious. Occasionally, however, these stressful thoughts rise to the surface and cause conflicts in her life, such that every time her husband comes home from work and pretends that nothing has happened, she feels angry and resentful.

According to Freud's theory, the woman might behave in several specific ways to avoid dealing with this conflict. She might act in the exact opposite way of how you would expect her to act and be exceptionally kind to her husband. She might completely block out the memory of her husband's infidelity. Or she might even vent her anger on someone other than her husband.

The goal of Freud's treatment was to make these methods of avoidance known to the patient, to free him or her from the problem. This process involved letting the patients talk in a free, open way about anything that was on their mind. Simultaneously, the therapist's job was to make interpretations about how the patient was feeling, the nature and origins of the problem, and the relationship that the patient had with the therapist. But at no point was the therapist supposed to offer the patient any direct advice or teach the patient coping skills to deal with the problem. Unfortunately, this type of treatment often took months or even years to help the patient. And although many thousands of people did find relief using Freud's treatment over the years, some therapists wondered whether there was a more direct way to help their patients.

COGNITIVE THERAPY

Then in the 1950s and '60s, a revolution took place in the field of psychology. Separately, both psychiatrist Aaron Beck and psychologist Albert Ellis discovered that something other than the repression of unconscious conflicts was causing their patients' problems. The cause of their problems was the patients' own thoughts, and many patients were fully aware that they were having them—many of their thoughts weren't unconscious at all. For example, they found that someone who continually thought, "I'm no good; I'll always fail," often felt sad or anxious. Beck called these types of thoughts automatic thoughts, and they play a central role in what's come to be known as cognitive therapy.

Automatic thoughts are self-critical thoughts that you frequently think and say to yourself. They influence your mood, affect your behaviors, and sabotage your success. Other examples of automatic thoughts include those like "I don't deserve anything good to happen to me," and "Why bother trying? I'm just going to fail." Much of the work in cognitive therapy involves challenging your automatic thoughts. A key way to do so is by using the Challenge Your Unhelpful Thinking Styles worksheet, which you'll learn about in chapter 5. That worksheet helps you to look for information that both supports and contradicts these automatic thoughts, and then it helps you to create a more balanced thought. For example, if you struggle with anxiety and you habitually think to yourself, "Nothing I do is ever good enough," you'll look for examples of this being true and examples of it not being true from your life. Then, hopefully, you'll be able to come up with a more balanced thought that eases your anxiety, such as "Even though I don't do everything perfectly, I'm still capable of doing most things pretty well."

Beck also identified several common cognitive errors that people often make, which are equally important in fueling their mental health problems. One example is called *overgeneralizing*. When you make this cognitive error, you make broad negative conclusions about your ability to function in life based on limited situations; for example, "I got one bad review at work. I'll probably screw up my relationship with my wife, too. I can't do anything right." You'll learn more about these cognitive errors in chapter 5.

BEHAVIOR THERAPY

Similar to cognitive therapy, behavior therapy was equally revolutionizing to the field of psychology in the 1950s and '60s, with the work of psychologist B. F. Skinner, but the foundation of the treatment began long before that. At the beginning of the twentieth century, early behavioral theory was largely influenced by the work of the famous Russian physiologist and Nobel Prize winner Ivan Pavlov. Pavlov discovered that the dogs used in his research experiments salivated both when they saw their food and when they heard the ringing of a bell that announced the arrival of their food. In the dog's brain, the association of the food and the bell had become the same, and therefore both elicited the same response. Pavlov's work became known as *classical conditioning*.

In the 1950s, Skinner used techniques that were similar to Pavlov's and brought behavior theory to the forefront of psychology. Skinner discovered that he could use forms of reward and punishment to shape the behavior of animals, and later of humans, in a technique called *operant conditioning*. Both Skinner and Pavlov greatly influenced the learning theories of what later became known as behavior therapy.

As its name implies, *behavior therapy* focuses on the way that dysfunctional behaviors lead to mental health problems. One of the main beliefs of this treatment is that your actions and reactions are largely learned. Some behaviors are actively reinforced and rewarded with things like food and money, while others are learned by watching and imitating people. Overall, the goal of behavior therapy is to help you learn new actions that can improve your life.

The methods used in behavior therapy will depend on the nature of your problem, but often they include relaxation exercises, training in assertive communication skills, and problem-solving skills. You'll also be asked to record your behaviors during the week, in order to observe your progress.

Depending on your problem, you might also need to engage in activities that often seem challenging. Many people avoid certain activities, which only results in making their problems more difficult. For example, a person with avoidant personality disorder who neglects calling friends and then feels lonely will need to overcome this fear eventually. The process of confronting feared situations in a safe and systematic way is called *exposure*. It requires you to make a list of your feared situations and then confront them, either in real life or in your imagination, beginning with the least fearful situation and working your way up to the most difficult. The goal of this treatment is to help you successfully confront your fears in a safe, progressive way and, by so doing, to help you realize that nothing bad or dangerous will happen to you. You'll learn more about this in chapter 11.

COGNITIVE BEHAVIORAL THERAPY

As its name implies, cognitive behavioral therapy is a form of treatment that combines elements of both cognitive and behavior therapies. The components of the treatment taken from cognitive therapy will help you to examine the way your thoughts affect your mental health. And the components taken from behavior therapy will help you to investigate the way that your actions influence your life and your interactions with others. When used as part of a single treatment for personality disorders, CBT examines the way you can change both your thoughts and behaviors in order to improve your life.

Overall, CBT is a very effective treatment for many mental health issues, including depression, anxiety, phobias, panic disorder, post-traumatic stress disorder, and obsessive-compulsive disorder.[51] And although the number of studies has been few,[52] research also supports the use of CBT to treat personality disorders,[53] even when the treatment is limited to a brief number of sessions.[54]

However, the majority of experts will agree that the most effective CBT treatment for your personality disorder is likely to be more intensive and take longer than the treatment for other mental health problems like depression.[55] Also, its success will depend on your commitment to the treatment.[56]

CBT TREATMENT FOR PERSONALITY DISORDERS

In general, the CBT skills in this workbook are the same ones that are used to successfully treat other problems like depression and anxiety. Most of the skills used in this workbook are based on the recommendations of Aaron Beck, Arthur Freeman, and their associates, who wrote a CBT treatment manual for therapists called *Cognitive Therapy of Personality Disorders*.[36] According to this esteemed group of clinicians, the CBT treatment of personality disorders should help you do the following:

1. Get reactivated in life.

2. Challenge and correct self-defeating thoughts.

3. Develop healthier core beliefs.

4. Learn stress-reduction and relaxation techniques.

5. Engage in real-life exposure to feared situations.

6. Practice assertive communication skills.

In addition, three other skills have been included in this workbook to make your treatment even more effective. They will help you do the following:

1. Develop problem-solving skills.

2. Practice coping imagery.

3. Prevent relapse.

IN CONCLUSION

Cognitive behavioral therapy can be a very effective treatment for many people struggling with personality disorders, if they are willing to make the commitment to build new habits and learn new coping skills. However, many clients are often looking for a quick fix. Frequently, they want to know how long the treatment will take to solve their problems and how much time they need to invest in the process. The answer, unfortunately, is different for each person.

Remember that you've probably been struggling with these problems for many years, and over that time you've developed cognitive and behavioral habits that have become fairly rigid. Therefore, the treatment might take weeks, months, or even years to make certain changes. But please don't let that dissuade you from committing to the process. The truth is that changing any habit often takes a long time.

In order to begin the process of changing your habits, start now by engaging in new activities in your life using the techniques you will find in chapter 4.

PART II

Specific Cognitive Therapy Skills

Get Reactivated in Life

One of the initial steps of the CBT treatment for personality disorders is to help you get reactivated. Many people with personality disorders avoid doing necessary and interesting activities and often isolate themselves from the rest of the world. However, avoidance only deepens the problem. If you're already not feeling good about your life and then you stop doing the activities that you enjoy, you'll probably feel even worse.

For example, remember Dwight from chapter 1? He struggled with dependent personality disorder. Very often, Dwight thought to himself, "I'm not capable of doing anything without my girlfriend's help." Not only did this thought cause Dwight to feel distressed, but it also meant that nothing got done unless his girlfriend was around to help him. His bills didn't get paid, his house never got cleaned, and he could never decide what to eat. As a result, not only did he feel dependent on his girlfriend (and others), but he also had bill collectors calling him, his house was always messy, and he frequently felt hungry.

Similarly, Ava, who struggled with avoidant personality disorder, frequently had the thought "I'm not as smart or as pretty as other people." Not only did this thought make her feel lonely and inferior, but she also avoided most situations when there was the possibility that others would judge or criticize her. She didn't go out with colleagues after work, she had few friends, and she frequently avoided going places where other people would be around, like the shopping mall. As a result, Ava's actions made her feel even lonelier, and often she didn't have the items that she needed or wanted.

EXERCISE: Avoidance Identification

Identify some of the chores, tasks, and pleasurable activities that you've been avoiding, putting off, or neglecting recently, and note any effect this has had on your life:

_____

_____

As you can see, getting reactivated is one of the most important initial steps in the treatment of personality disorders. Getting reactivated in life can help you do those daily activities and chores that you've long put off, as well as help you to begin scheduling pleasurable activities back into your life.

There's no denying that getting reactivated in your life is probably going to be hard work. If it were easy, you'd already be doing it. However, it's a necessary step to take in order to start moving your life in a new direction. For many people struggling with personality disorders, it's often helpful to use a Weekly Activity Schedule, both to keep a record of what you usually do during the week and to plan new activities that you'd like to accomplish.

EXERCISE: Weekly Activity Schedule

To begin this exercise, make at least ten photocopies of the following blank Weekly Activity Schedule. As you'll see, the columns on the form are divided into the days of the week, and the rows are divided into several blocks of hours. Over the following week, do your best to record what you do throughout the day. If you can, keep a copy of the form with you to record activities after you've done them. However, if this is too difficult, at least record your activities at the end of each day. Don't wait until the end of the week because it will be too difficult to recall what you were doing hour by hour and how your activities made you feel.

Remember, this activity is only for you; it is not for anyone else. No one will grade or judge you on what you have or haven't done. The purpose of this first activity is to be as honest with yourself as possible and to complete an inventory of how you spend your time throughout the week. Who knows what you'll discover? For example, you might find that you spend a lot of time:

- By yourself
- Waiting for other people to do things for you
- Trying to please other people
- Worrying about other people
- Doing tasks that you don't like to do
- Worrying over the details of a project
- Harming yourself in some way

You are the only one who will be able to determine if your time is spent doing the things you need to do to lead a fulfilling life. So do your best to complete the schedule as accurately as possible. As an extra challenge, for each activity that you record, note the levels of pleasure and mastery that doing the activities gave to you. Also, if you can, note whether you were avoiding some other activity.

Pleasure is the sense of enjoyment you experience when doing an activity. You can rate it from 0 (no pleasure) to 10 (extreme pleasure). Many people with personality disorders are surprised to discover that their weekly activities provide them with little or no enjoyment, which makes it important to schedule pleasurable activities back into your life.

Mastery is the sense that you are accomplishing something that's important to you. You can rate it from 0 (no sense of accomplishment) to 10 (extreme sense of accomplishment). Without activities that give you a sense of accomplishment, life sometimes feels dull or meaningless. For that reason, it's important to have these types of activities as part of your life too; and you may need to schedule them as well.

And, finally, if during the day you become aware that you're avoiding an activity, note that in your schedule. For example, if you're watching television when you are really avoiding washing the dishes, write that on the form. Again, the purpose of this exercise is to discover how you spend your time and to learn what you can do differently. After you've spent a week recording your daily activities, move on to the next exercise.

For more ideas about how to fill out a Weekly Activity Schedule, refer to Britney's example, which follows the blank schedule you are to photocopy and use. (Remember, Britney is struggling with borderline personality disorder.) Note the way Britney recorded pleasurable activities with a P, mastery activities with an M, and avoidance activities with an A. After completing this exercise, she noticed that she had not engaged in many activities that provided her with a sense of either accomplishment (mastery) or enjoyment (pleasure), and so she needed to schedule some activities into her life that would do that. She also recognized that she had spent much of her free time watching television, but that she really hadn't enjoyed it. Clearly, watching television was just a way for her to avoid doing her schoolwork and to kill time.

Weekly Activity Schedule

Note: Pleasure = P, Mastery = M, and Avoidance = A

Time	Monday	Tuesday	Wednesday	Thursday	Friday	Saturday	Sunday
Early Morning							
9-10 a.m.							
10-11 a.m.							
11-12 a.m.							
12-1 p.m.							
1-2 p.m.							
2-3 p.m.							
3-4 p.m.							
4-5 p.m.							
5-6 p.m.							
6-7 p.m.							
7-8 p.m.							
Late Evening							

Weekly Activity Schedule—Britney's Example

Note Pleasure = (P), Mastery = (M), and Avoidance = (A)

Time	Monday	Tuesday	Wednesday	Thursday	Friday	Saturday	Sunday
Early Morning	Sleep	Sleep	Sleep	School @ 8 a.m. M: 2	School @ 7:30 a.m. M: 3	Sleep	Sleep
9-10 a.m.	Get to work M: 4	Get to work M: 4	Get to work M: 4	Economics class	Psychology class	Walk w/Tracy P: 5	Sleep
10-11 a.m.	Make calls @ work M: 3	Make calls @ work M: 3	Make calls @ work M: 3	Economics class	Psychology class	Coffee w/Tracy P: 4	Farmer's market P: 7
11-12 a.m.	Billing M: 6	Meeting M: 3	Billing M: 6	Economics class M: 6	Psychology class M: 5	Back in bed A: Calling Jason	Café
12-1 p.m.	Lunch w/Tracy P: 6	Lunch w/Tracy P: 7	Lunch w/Tracy P: 3	Walk around campus A: Studying	Lunch and reading P: 2 M: 3	Back in bed A: Calling Jason	Café P: 4
1-2 p.m.	Work with Margaret on project M: 4	Browse Internet A: billing	Review week's sales M: 6	Library to study M: 5	Library to study M: 4	Lunch P: 5	Television P: 5
2-3 p.m.	Talk to Bob about accounts payable. M: 3	Sales meeting M: 5	Browse Internet P: 3 A: billing	English Lit. class	World History class	Talked to Jason P: 8	Television P: 5
3-4 p.m.	Write report M: 4	Talked w/Margaret P: 5	Browse Internet P: 3 A: calling customers	English Lit. class	World History class	Study M: 6	Early dinner
4-5 p.m.	Review report w/ Gary M: 4	Reorder supplies M: 7	Phone customers M: 5	English Lit. class M: 4	World History class M: 3	Study M: 6	Television
5-6 p.m.	Drive home M: 2	Drive home M: 2	Drive home M: 2	Bike home P: 5	Bike home P: 4	Television	Television
6-7 p.m.	Dinner @ home w/ Jason	Dinner @ home alone P: 4	Dinner w/Jason	Dinner alone P: 3	Dinner P: 5	Television	Television
7-8 p.m.	Dinner @ home w/ Jason P: 9	Television P: 5 A: schoolwork	Dinner w/Jason	Television P: 4 A: schoolwork	Movie @ home alone P: 4	Television P: 3 A: schoolwork	Television P: 3 A: schoolwork
Late Evening	Bed at 12	Bed at 11	Dinner w/Jason P: 10	Bed at 12	Bed at 1 a.m.	Bed at 11	Bed at 10

WEEKLY ACTIVITY SCHEDULE—RESULTS

After recording your activities for a week, look for any noticeable results. Did you have many pleasurable activities in your life? Did you have any activities that brought you a sense of accomplishment? Were there many activities you avoided by doing something else? Would you say that this was an example of a typical week for you, or does your life look very different from this most of the time?

Remember, life isn't going to be meaningful and pleasurable all the time. We all have days and even weeks that seem to be empty of either pleasure or satisfaction. But if that's the way your life feels most of the time, it might mean that in some way your life is out of balance. Perhaps you're working too much or spending too much time going over the details of a project that has already been completed. Maybe you're spending too much time worrying about what others are going to do instead of making plans for yourself. Or perhaps you've put off making plans because you're not sure how they will turn out and you want everything to be perfect; and as a result, you haven't done anything.

Whatever the reason, many people with personality disorders get stuck in habitual patterns of behavior that lead them to do the same things over and over again, even if those things are unpleasant or unsatisfying. The purpose of this exercise is to observe your patterns and then to do something differently. If your old behaviors haven't been giving you satisfaction, there's little reason to think that they'll be any better in the future.

EXERCISE: Making Sense of the Results

In the space below, record your thoughts about the Weekly Activity Schedule. What did you notice? Were there enough pleasurable and satisfying experiences throughout the week? Was there too much avoidance? What needs to change?

_____

_____

_____

_____

_____

_____

_____

_____

_____

PLEASURABLE ACTIVITIES

Did you observe that you don't have many pleasurable activities in your weekly life? If so, you might benefit by making time for such activities. Many people who lack pleasure in their lives say, "What should I do? I don't know many pleasurable things to do." So the big list of pleasurable activities is provided below to help you deal with this issue. The list includes over one hundred activities for you to choose from. Mark the activities that you'd like to schedule into your life, or you can even create a list of your own. These can be activities that you once enjoyed doing or new things that you'd like to try.

The Big List of Pleasurable Activities

Check the activities you're willing to do and then add any others you can think of that you might also like to do:

- ☐ Talk to a friend on the telephone.
- ☐ Go out and visit a friend.
- ☐ Invite a friend to visit you at your home.
- ☐ Text message your friends.
- ☐ Spend time with your family.
- ☐ Organize a party.
- ☐ Exercise.
- ☐ Lift weights.
- ☐ Do yoga, tai chi, or Pilates, or take classes to learn.
- ☐ Stretch your muscles.
- ☐ Go for a long walk in a park or somewhere else that's peaceful.
- ☐ Go outside and watch the clouds.
- ☐ Go for a jog.
- ☐ Ride your bike.
- ☐ Go for a swim.
- ☐ Go hiking.
- ☐ Do something exciting, like surfing, rock climbing, skiing, skydiving, or kayaking, or learn how to do one of these sports.
- ☐ Go to your local playground and join a game being played or watch a game.
- ☐ Go play something you can do by yourself if no one else is around, like basketball, bowling, handball, miniature golf, billiards, or hitting a tennis ball against the wall.
- ☐ Get a massage; this can also help to soothe your emotions.
- ☐ Get out of your house, even if you just sit outside in the fresh air.
- ☐ Go for a drive in your car or take a ride on public transportation.
- ☐ Plan a trip to a place you've never been before.
- ☐ Sleep or take a nap.
- ☐ Eat chocolate (it's good for you!) or eat something else you really like.

- ☐ Eat your favorite ice cream.
- ☐ Cook your favorite dish or meal.
- ☐ Cook a recipe that you've never tried before.
- ☐ Take a cooking class.
- ☐ Go out for something to eat.
- ☐ Go outside and play with your pet.
- ☐ Borrow a friend's dog and take it to the park.
- ☐ Give your pet a bath.
- ☐ Go outside and watch the birds and other living creatures.
- ☐ Find something amusing to do, like reading the Sunday comics.
- ☐ Watch a funny movie. (Start collecting funny movies to watch when you're feeling overwhelmed with pain.)
- ☐ Go to a movie theater and watch whatever's playing.
- ☐ Watch television.
- ☐ Listen to the radio.
- ☐ Go to a sporting event, like a baseball or football game.
- ☐ Play a game with a friend.
- ☐ Play solitaire.
- ☐ Play video games.
- ☐ Go online to chat.
- ☐ Visit your favorite websites.
- ☐ Visit crazy websites and start keeping a list of them.
- ☐ Create your own website.
- ☐ Create your own online blog.
- ☐ Join an Internet dating service.
- ☐ Sell something you don't want on the Internet.
- ☐ Buy something on the Internet.
- ☐ Do a puzzle with a lot of pieces.
- ☐ Go shopping.
- ☐ Get a haircut.
- ☐ Go to a spa.

- ☐ Go to a library.
- ☐ Go to a bookstore and read.
- ☐ Go to your favorite café for coffee or tea.
- ☐ Visit a museum or local art gallery.
- ☐ Go to the mall or the park and watch other people; try to imagine what they're thinking.
- ☐ Pray or meditate.
- ☐ Go to your church, synagogue, temple, or other place of worship.
- ☐ Join a group at your place of worship.
- ☐ Write a letter to God.
- ☐ Call a family member you haven't spoken to in a long time.
- ☐ Learn a new language.
- ☐ Sing or learn how to sing.
- ☐ Play a musical instrument or learn how to play one.
- ☐ Write a song.
- ☐ Listen to some upbeat, happy music. (Start collecting happy songs for times when you're feeling overwhelmed.)
- ☐ Turn on some loud music and dance in your room.
- ☐ Memorize lines from your favorite movie, play, or song.
- ☐ Make a movie or video with your camcorder.
- ☐ Take photographs.
- ☐ Join a public speaking group and write a speech.
- ☐ Participate in a local theater group.
- ☐ Sing in a local choir.
- ☐ Join a club.
- ☐ Plant a garden.
- ☐ Do some outdoor work around the house.
- ☐ Knit, crochet, or sew—or learn how to.
- ☐ Make a scrapbook with pictures.
- ☐ Paint your nails.
- ☐ Change your hair color.
- ☐ Take a bubble bath or shower.
- ☐ Work on your car, truck, motorcycle, or bicycle.

- ☐ Sign up for a class that excites you at a local college, adult school, or online.
- ☐ Read your favorite book, magazine, paper, or poem.
- ☐ Read a trashy celebrity magazine.
- ☐ Write a letter to a friend or family member.
- ☐ Write a list of the things you like about yourself.
- ☐ Write a poem, story, movie, or play about your life or someone else's life.
- ☐ Write in your journal or diary about what happened to you today.
- ☐ Write a loving letter to yourself when you're feeling good, and keep it with you to read when you're feeling upset.
- ☐ Make a list of ten things you're good at or that you like about yourself when you're feeling good, and keep it with you to read when you're feeling upset.
- ☐ Draw a picture.
- ☐ Paint a picture with a brush or your fingers.
- ☐ Share intimate experiences with someone you care about.
- ☐ Make a list of the people you admire and want to be like—they can be real or fictional people throughout history. Describe what you admire about them.
- ☐ Write a story about the craziest, funniest, or sexiest thing that ever happened to you.
- ☐ Make a list of ten things you would like to do before you die.
- ☐ Make a list of ten celebrities you would like to be friends with and describe why.
- ☐ Write a letter to someone who has made your life better and tell the person why. (You don't have to send the letter if you don't want to.)
- ☐ Create your own list of pleasurable activities.
- ☐ Other ideas: _____
- ☐ _____
- ☐ _____
- ☐ _____

MASTERY ACTIVITIES

Follow the same suggestions for reviewing the mastery activities in your daily life. Do you engage in many activities during the week that give you a sense of satisfaction? If not, you might benefit from scheduling some of these activities into your life. These activities can range from simple chores like doing the dishes to more complicated activities like completing a big project at work. Some of the suggestions might repeat ideas from the previous list, but that's okay. Everyone gets pleasure and satisfaction from different kinds of activities.

The Big List of Mastery Activities

Check the activities you're willing to do and then add any others that you can think of:

- ☐ Spend uninterrupted time with your family, spouse, children, or friends.
- ☐ Go shopping for items you need.
- ☐ Go shopping for items you want.
- ☐ Go to the bank.
- ☐ Pay your bills.
- ☐ Balance your checking account.
- ☐ Go to work (if you've been avoiding it).
- ☐ Finish a task at work that you've been avoiding, delaying, or spending too much time completing.
- ☐ Ask for help with a task at work.
- ☐ Assign a work task to someone else.
- ☐ Seek guidance from a supervisor at work.
- ☐ Challenge yourself by completing a difficult task without asking for help from anyone else.
- ☐ Help your child with his or her homework.
- ☐ Help your child with bedtime activities.
- ☐ Wash the dishes.
- ☐ Wash your clothes or take them to the cleaner.
- ☐ Put away your clothes.
- ☐ Fix something that's in need of repair.
- ☐ Clean something that's dirty.
- ☐ Take a shower or a bath.
- ☐ Clean and organize a messy shelf, desk, or kitchen counter.
- ☐ Prepare a healthy meal for yourself or someone else.
- ☐ Write a letter or e-mail to someone you've been thinking about or avoiding.
- ☐ Investigate your spiritual or religious beliefs and join a group with similar beliefs if you want to.
- ☐ Pray, meditate, or just sit still for as long as you can.
- ☐ Take care of the way you look and feel; get a haircut or a manicure if necessary.
- ☐ Engage in some type of creative activity, like painting, drawing, or writing.
- ☐ Get needed maintenance and repairs completed on your car or other vehicle.
- ☐ Start keeping a personal journal to record your thoughts in.
- ☐ Plant a garden or work in your garden.
- ☐ Clean up the interior of your home.
- ☐ Complete some small repair to your home.
- ☐ Organize some area of your home or work.
- ☐ Redecorate a room in your home or office.
- ☐ Spend time appreciating nature; go to a park, a lake, or the woods if necessary.
- ☐ Visit someplace that is special to you, such as a city or a monument.

- ☐ Take care of your physical health; visit a medical professional for a checkup or a needed visit.
- ☐ Take care of your mental health; visit a mental health care professional for therapy or assistance.
- ☐ Get involved with your local community in a way that is meaningful to you.
- ☐ Complete work around the outside of your home.
- ☐ Volunteer to help an organization that you care about.
- ☐ Make a difficult business call that you've been avoiding.
- ☐ Schedule a difficult business meeting that you've been avoiding.
- ☐ Return a telephone call to someone you've been avoiding.
- ☐ Complete an errand that you've been avoiding.
- ☐ Get dressed up for an appropriate occasion, like going to work or visiting someone.
- ☐ Resolve a conflict that's been bothering you or interfering with your life.
- ☐ Provide needed care for your pets.
- ☐ Enroll in a class or for some special training that you need.
- ☐ Do your best to solve a problem that you've been avoiding.
- ☐ Go for a walk.
- ☐ Exercise.
- ☐ Stretch your muscles.
- ☐ Help someone you care about.
- ☐ Other ideas: _____
- ☐ _____
- ☐ _____
- ☐ _____

EXERCISE: Schedule Pleasurable and Mastery Activities

Now that you've reviewed your weekly activities and identified some pleasurable and mastery activities that you'd like to engage in, it's time to schedule those activities into your week. To begin, look at the Weekly Activity Schedule that you completed and note the days when you are in need of more pleasure or accomplishment. Then identify the times when you could schedule some of those activities into your daily routines.

Be realistic when scheduling your activities. It might be too complicated to schedule an entire week of activities in advance. Instead schedule them one or two days in advance. Also, if you work eight or nine hours a day or you attend school, you probably can't schedule a pleasurable activity like "go to the movies" into the middle of your day. However, you might be able to schedule a walk during lunchtime. And in the beginning, don't take on more than one mastery activity per day, especially if it is a new activity. Trying to do more than one might become too challenging. Later on, after you've begun to feel comfortable with the new activity, you can try scheduling additional mastery activities.

When scheduling activities, be aware that you might be unable to complete a pleasurable or mastery activity in one hour or even in one day. You might have to break some activities into smaller tasks to complete them. For example, if one of your pleasurable goals is to visit Washington, D.C., and you live in Dallas, Texas, you probably need to do some planning for the trip. Or if your mastery goal is to redecorate your apartment, most likely you will need to complete it over the course of several days or weeks; and you may be able to dedicate only one hour a day to the task. That's okay. Remember, the goal of this activity is to begin making changes to your life that will make life feel more satisfying and fulfilling to you.

For an additional challenge, try predicting how much pleasure or sense of accomplishment each activity will give to you. Many people with personality disorders anticipate that they will not enjoy an activity very much or take much satisfaction in it. To see if your anticipations are correct, try making a prediction about each activity. Then after you've completed the activity, record what your actual level of pleasure or accomplishment was and see whether your prediction was accurate. If you notice that your new activities make you feel better than you anticipated feeling, this might help you confront other difficult activities in the future and stand up to the self-critical thoughts that tell you to give up and not to try anything new.

Try scheduling activities for at least the next four to eight weeks—and you can continue doing this while you're learning other skills. It will probably take that long for you to notice the benefits of making these changes and to begin engaging in these types of activities in a more natural way, without having to schedule them.

Britney's Example of Scheduling Pleasurable and Mastery Activities

An example of how Britney scheduled new activities into her week follows. She started by noting the times in her schedule when she was engaged in activities that were neither pleasurable nor fulfilling. Next she chose new activities from both Big Lists. Then she scheduled those activities into her daily life. Finally, she made predictions about how much pleasure or sense of mastery those activities would provide her with. (Her predictions are underlined.)

Weekly Activity Schedule—Britney's Example

Note: Pleasure = P, Mastery = M, and Avoidance = A

Time	Monday	Tuesday	Wednesday	Thursday	Friday	Saturday	Sunday
Early Morning							
9-10 a.m.							Clean apartment Predict: M=3 Actual: M=8
10-11 a.m.							
11-12 a.m.						Study for class Predict: M=4 Actual: M=6	
12-1 p.m.	Short walk after lunch Predict: P=5 Actual: P=6			Study for class Predict: M=3 Actual: M=5	Study for class Predict: M=3 Actual: M=5		Work in garden Predict: P=5 Actual: P=9
1-2 p.m.		Complete billing Predict: M=4 Actual: M=6					
2-3 p.m.							
3-4 p.m.			Phone customers Predict: M=3 Actual: M=4			Take a walk in park Predict: P=4 Actual: P=7	
4-5 p.m.							
5-6 p.m.		Dinner w/Tracy Predict: P=5 Actual: P=7	Shopping Predict: P=6 Actual: P=7				
6-7 p.m.	Food shopping Predict: M=3 Actual: M=4			Dinner w/Jason Predict: P=6 Actual: P=9			
7-8 p.m.					Movie w/Jason Predict: P=7 Actual: P=8		
Late Evening							

MAKING TIME

In the twenty-first century, we all lead busy lives. There's always something else that we could (or should) be doing. That's why it's important for you to find some time in your life for the activities that make you feel happy, fulfilled, and satisfied. When you first start scheduling new activities into your week, you might have to cut out some unnecessary ones, such as watching television or browsing the Internet, to make the time for more important activities, such as spending time with your family and completing necessary chores.

Scheduling activities may also require you to become a researcher. That is, you may have to try out a number of different activities before you discover which ones provide you with the most pleasure and sense of accomplishment. That's okay. Remember, the point of this exercise is to do something different. By definition, people who have personality disorders are struggling with long-standing, dysfunctional habits that interfere with their lives. If anything is going to improve in your life, you're going to have to take a leap of faith and try something new. Start with something small, like completing a task, before you tackle something big, like returning a phone call to someone you don't like. Set yourself up for a successful experience and you'll be more likely to take on bigger challenges in the future. And remember, write down your activities on your schedule. Recording them in writing increases the likelihood that you'll follow through with your plans.

USE COPING STATEMENTS

If you're still having trouble committing yourself to new activities, try using a coping statement. A *coping statement* is a little phrase that can help you to:

- Get motivated

- Feel inspired

- Remind yourself of your ability to handle difficult situations

- Remind you of your past successes

- Develop an attitude of acceptance

Whenever you're in doubt about your ability to take on a new challenge, change your schedule, or try something new, repeat one of the phrases below either silently or aloud a few times. Let the positive, self-affirming message sink in, and then try confronting the challenge again.

Find a phrase below that makes you feel hopeful about your ability to succeed, or you can create your own coping statement:

- "I don't have to do the activity perfectly; just trying something new is a success."

- "I can do this; it's okay to feel scared or anxious, but I won't let it stop me."

- "This feeling is uncomfortable, but I can do this."

- "I've succeeded in the past when I've taken on challenges like this."

- "This isn't dangerous; I'm just trying something new."

- "I need to take a leap of faith and believe that everything will be okay."

- "This is just anxiety (or doubt); I won't let it stop me."

- "My doubt will eventually pass."

- "I'm just researching activities that might improve my life; I don't have to commit to anything I don't really like to do."

- "Nothing will change unless I'm willing to try something new."

- "I don't need these negative thoughts; I can choose to think positively."

Now create your own coping thoughts:

_____

_____

_____

_____

IN CONCLUSION

Many people with personality disorders get stuck in habitual patterns of behavior that often make their lives feel dull and unrewarding. Breaking these habits is very important. It can be difficult, but it's not impossible. Sometimes it's just necessary to observe how you're spending your time and then plan new, fulfilling activities.

Do your best to commit to scheduling these new activities for at least four to eight weeks, and observe any potential benefits they've had in your life. Does your life feel more fulfilling as a result of doing these new activities? Do you experience more pleasure in your life? If your answer to either question is yes, then keep scheduling similar new activities. If your answer is no, don't give up. Perhaps you're not engaging in the best activities for yourself. Maybe you are scheduling activities that you think you should enjoy or activities that other people like. Be honest with yourself and choose activities that you think are pleasurable and fulfilling, and you'll be more likely to experience a sense of satisfaction.

CHAPTER 5

Challenge and Correct Self-Defeating Thoughts

Perhaps the most important step of the cognitive behavioral treatment for personality disorders is to challenge and correct self-defeating thoughts. These thoughts are often the cause of many distressing feelings and unhealthy behaviors. At the heart of CBT is the belief that your thoughts, feelings, and behaviors all interact and influence each other (and feelings can be either emotional or physical). Take a look at this diagram:

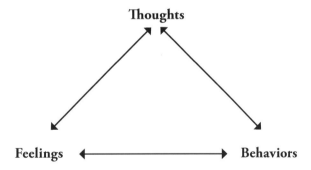

This shows how your thoughts can influence your feelings and behaviors, as well as how your thoughts can be affected by your feelings and behaviors.

Let's look at an example. Anthony struggled with antisocial personality disorder. One day, he lost his favorite watch (a behavior). Anthony felt upset (an emotional feeling), and then he thought to himself, "I bet my friend Paul stole it" (a thought). This thought made him feel angry (another emotion) and tight in his chest (a physical feeling). So he went to Paul's house and got into an argument with him (a behavior) and later felt betrayed (an emotion). From this example, do you see how emotions can be both the result and the cause of your thoughts and behaviors?

This pattern can become a vicious cycle of upsetting emotions, self-defeating thoughts, and dysfunctional behaviors. However, this cycle also can lead to more fulfilling emotional experiences if you learn to challenge your self-defeating thoughts. For example, maybe after Anthony lost his watch (a behavior) and felt upset (an emotion), he could have challenged the thought that Paul stole it with another thought, such as, "Paul has never stolen anything from me in the past, I don't think he would steal anything from me." Then he might have been able to figure out how to find his watch (another thought) and continue his day, feeling more at ease (an emotion). Or after feeling upset about losing his watch, perhaps he could have gone for a long walk (a behavior), which would have made him feel soothed (an emotion). There are many different kinds of coping thoughts and behaviors that Anthony could have used to prevent getting caught in a cycle of distressing thoughts, emotions, and behaviors, but he had never learned any of them.

THE GOALS OF THIS CHAPTER

This chapter will help you identify the ways in which your thoughts are affecting your feelings and behaviors, and it will also help you identify the ways in which your thoughts are contributing to your personality disorder. Most importantly, however, this chapter will teach you how to challenge and change some of those thoughts, in order to break free of your habits. Specifically, this chapter will teach you:

- How to recognize your distressing automatic thoughts

- How to record your automatic thoughts in a Thought Journal

- How to recognize and challenge unhelpful thinking styles

- How to challenge your automatic thoughts by examining your past experiences

The information and skills you learn in this chapter will be crucial to you in chapter 6, where you will learn how to identify and change your negative core beliefs about yourself and the world.

This is a long chapter because it is one of the most important in the book. This one chapter might take you several weeks or even months to work through, but that's okay. Take your time and make sure you understand the material. Work through the exercises in the order that they appear. If you try to skip ahead in this chapter, you can easily get lost. While you are working with the material in this chapter, also continue to schedule and engage in pleasurable and mastery activities, as you did in chapter 4.

AUTOMATIC THOUGHTS

The initial step of challenging the way you think is to observe your automatic thoughts. *Automatic thoughts* are self-critical thoughts that people think and say to themselves that sabotage their attempts at success and happiness. Imagine listening all day to a radio station that only criticizes you, judges your actions, and tells you what to do. This is very similar to what many people experience with their automatic thoughts. Here are some common examples of automatic thoughts:

- I don't deserve anything good happening to me.

- Why bother trying? I'm just going to fail anyway.

- I'm incapable of doing anything by myself.

- I should always try to please other people.

- I must never make any mistakes.

- Life isn't fair.

- Nobody likes me.

You can be aware or completely unaware that you're having thoughts like these. In either case, they'll probably make you feel sad, anxious, frustrated, angry, or hopeless. Or after having a thought like this, you might engage in some kind of behavior that interferes with your life, such as avoiding necessary chores, getting angry at others, or physically hurting yourself.

Characteristics of Automatic Thoughts

Automatic thoughts often share common characteristics, which makes them easier to identify.[57]

1. **Automatic thoughts are often repetitive**. This means you'll often have automatic thoughts throughout the day or week. It also means that your automatic thoughts will frequently share a common theme, such as criticizing yourself or others. For example, people struggling with paranoid personalities often have thoughts that other people are trying to harm them, while people with schizotypal personalities frequently think that they don't fit in with the rest of society.

2. **Automatic thoughts often catastrophize**. This means that you'll exaggerate the worst-case scenario of anything that goes wrong or could go wrong. For example, many people struggling with obsessive-compulsive personalities think that if they make a mistake, no matter how small it is, they'll be severely punished. Similarly, people who have histrionic personalities often think that if other people aren't paying attention to them, they'll be abandoned.

3. **Automatic thoughts are experienced as strict rules to be followed**. This means that such thoughts frequently use words like "should," "ought," "never," "always," or "must." Often these rules develop early in life and serve some purpose. But when maintained into adulthood, they can become less helpful or interfere with your life. For example, people struggling with dependent personalities often have the thought, "I must rely on other people for help," while people with narcissistic personalities think, "Other people should pay me the respect I deserve."

4. **Automatic thoughts can occur very quickly.** This means that they can appear as brief images, a few words, a sense of a situation, or a brief memory of a past event. For example, people struggling with schizoid personality might have the thought "I'm alone" or see an image of themselves alone. People with avoidant personalities might have the thought "I'll fail" or recall a brief memory of themselves being criticized.

Examples of Automatic Thoughts

Although each person's automatic thoughts will be unique, here are some generalized examples of what your automatic thoughts might be, based on the personality disorder(s) you're struggling with:

- **Antisocial personality disorder**: "The rules aren't meant for me." "I'm not responsible for anything." "Why should I care?" "Other people aren't as important as I am." "Other people get what they deserve."

- **Avoidant personality disorder**: "Everyone is always judging me." "Those people will criticize me." "I'm no good at making friends." "Other people are better than I am." "There's something wrong with me."

- **Borderline personality disorder**: "I don't want to be left alone." "No one understands me." "I always get hurt by others." "I'm worthless." "I'm empty inside."

- **Dependent personality disorder**: "I can't take care of myself." "I always need help." "I'm not smart enough." "If I do anything wrong, I'll be punished." "I shouldn't disagree with others."

- **Histrionic personality disorder**: "Other people should like me." "I need to be the center of attention." "I must please others." "If other people don't like me, I'll be left alone." "I need to be seductive in order to be liked."

- **Narcissistic personality disorder**: "I'm better than other people at most things." "Other people should compliment me more often." "I'm entitled to special privileges." "Very few people can truly understand me." "Other people should help me get what I want."

- **Obsessive-compulsive personality disorder**: "I need to keep everything in order." "I should never make a mistake." "If I mess up, I'll be punished." "I should always follow the rules." "I must always strive for perfection."

- **Paranoid personality disorder**: "I can't trust anyone." "People are trying to harm me." "I often feel threatened by others." "People will betray me if given the chance." "Others don't deserve my forgiveness."

- **Schizoid personality disorder**: "I'd rather be alone." "I don't know how to act around other people." "I'm very awkward in social situations." "Why bother trying? I'll just embarrass myself." "I don't need others' approval."

- **Schizotypal personality disorder**: "I don't fit in with the rest of society." "I don't know how to behave in social situations." "No one understands my special abilities." "I don't want to be alone." "People often try to take advantage of me."

- **Personality disorder not otherwise specified**: "Other people get special privileges that I don't." "Other people always have it easier than me." "Why should I care? No one helps me." "I'm never going to feel happy." "There's always something wrong with me."

EXERCISE: Your Own Thoughts

Were there any thoughts in the list above that you've had in the recent past? If you answer yes, record those thoughts below. Or you can record any similar automatic thoughts that you recognize:

_____

_____

_____

_____

_____

RECORDING YOUR OWN AUTOMATIC THOUGHTS

In addition to completing the exercise above, another way to recognize your automatic thoughts is to keep track of them throughout the day. Listening to your thoughts is often the first step in learning how to challenge them. This makes sense because many people aren't aware that they're thinking thousands of thoughts every day.

You'll probably be able to recognize your automatic thoughts most easily when they're connected to a distressing emotion, like anger, sadness, or worry. Remember, your thoughts, feelings, and behaviors all affect each other, but your thoughts are especially powerful. Very often, thoughts can make you feel a certain way instantaneously, such as when you have a memory of a pleasant vacation or of someone who has harmed you.

The point is that thoughts are powerful, even when they are too fast for you to recognize in your daily life. Sometimes we all get distressed or excited without knowing why, until we recognize what we were just thinking about. Some thoughts come quickly, as pictures or short phrases, while other thoughts resemble constant commentary and criticism from our "mind radios."

The Thought Journal

A Thought Journal is a useful tool to help you recognize your own thoughts. As you'll see, it's divided into three columns to help you identify: (1) the situation, (2) your feelings, and (3) your automatic thoughts. The situation is any event that triggers a distressing feeling or a critical automatic thought. Note that people frequently notice the distressing feeling before they notice their thought. So during the next week pay attention to any unpleasant emotions that you experience, such as sadness, anger, or worry. Then see if you can identify the situation and the thoughts that accompany it.

SCOTT'S EXAMPLE OF A THOUGHT JOURNAL

Look at Scott's Thought Journal. (Remember, Scott struggles with schizotypal personality disorder.) On Monday he had two experiences that brought up unpleasant emotions. First, he was late for work, which made him feel very worried. He also quickly recognized the thoughts that he was thinking: "I messed up again" and "I'll be fired." Later, when he brushed off a friend for lunch, he first identified what he was thinking, "Why do I keep avoiding people" and "She won't want to talk to me again," before he recognized that he felt guilty about brushing off his friend. In each of these cases, Scott recorded the experience as soon as possible. Then at least once a day throughout the week, he continued to record the situations that made him feel unpleasant, as well as the thoughts that he could identify.

PRACTICE USING THE THOUGHT JOURNAL

Before you begin using the Thought Journal, try a few practice experiences. For example, think back to a recent event that made you feel distressed or unpleasant. You might remember only that you felt bad. Do your best to relax, close your eyes, and try to remember what happened just before you felt that emotion. Also try to remember what you were thinking. Maybe your thought was only a word, like "alone." Try to expand that word into a full thought. Maybe it really indicated "I don't want to be alone." Or if you recognize an image, do your best to connect that image with a thought.

DIFFICULTIES IDENTIFYING THOUGHTS

Some people find it difficult to identify any thoughts at all. That's okay, especially in the beginning. Just do your best. At the very least, you might record each time you suspect that you had a thought, even if you don't know what it was. The more you practice, the easier the process will become.

And remember, no one is going to grade you on your thoughts, so be honest with yourself. You cannot change anything until you recognize what it is you're trying to change. Right now, you're examining your thoughts. If you start to notice that you have many critical thoughts about yourself or others, don't worry, you're not alone. Many people have similar critical thoughts. The exercises in this chapter will help you change some of those thoughts but, first, you must recognize and acknowledge what they are.

EXERCISE: Thought Journal

For the next three to four weeks, do your best to record at least one event in your Thought Journal every day. It's important that you write this information on the form, rather than trying to remember it, because writing it down:

- Will help you identify the situation, feelings, and automatic thoughts more easily.

- Will help you identify similar repetitious thoughts.

- You will need this information for later exercises.

- The more you practice, the more quickly you'll develop the ability to recognize your thoughts on a regular basis.

Thought Journal–Scott's Example

Situation	Feelings	Automatic Thoughts
When did the situation occur? Where were you? Who was involved? What happened?	Describe your feelings during the situation and rate their intensities from 0 to 10 (0 = no intensity, 10 = greatest intensity)	What were you thinking before you noticed the unpleasant feeling? Or what were you thinking during the emotional experience?
Mon., late for work	Worried (8)	"I messed up again." "I'll be fired."
Mon., brushed off Keri's invitation for lunch	Guilty (6)	"Why do I keep avoiding people?" "She won't want to talk to me again."
Tues., Ted asked me what I was doing	Suspicious (7)	"What does he care?" "Why are people always watching me?"
Wed., no one asked me to go out after work	Bothered (8)	"I always feel out of place." "No one likes me."
Thurs., the woman at the bus stop looked at me in a strange way	Angry (5) Suspicious (6)	"Why are people always looking at me that way?" "People should mind their own business."
Fri., Pete said he didn't understand me when I tried to explain what I saw in the sky last night	Alone (8) Bothered (9)	"No one ever understands me."
Sat., my girlfriend said she didn't have time for me today	Worried (5) Suspicious (7) Lonely (9)	"She always brushes me off whenever I want to do anything." "She probably wants to break up with me."
Sun., sitting in the park with other people around	Bothered (6) Weird (8)	"I think those people are looking at me." "Why don't people just leave me alone."
Sun., at home alone	Annoyed (7) Depressed (5)	"Why am I home alone again?" "I hate my job and I don't want to go to work tomorrow."

Thought Journal–Scott's Example

Situation	Feelings	Automatic Thoughts
When did the situation occur? Where were you? Who was involved? What happened?	Describe your feelings during the situation and rate their intensities from 0 to 10 (0 = no intensity, 10 = greatest intensity)	What were you thinking before you noticed the unpleasant feeling? Or what were you thinking during the emotional experience?

UNHELPFUL THINKING STYLES

Now that you've identified some of your automatic thoughts, and noticed any patterns of similar, repetitious thoughts, let's look at how those automatic thoughts can contribute to your problems. Psychiatrist Aaron Beck, the founder of cognitive therapy, identified some common unhelpful thinking styles when he studied people who were struggling with depression.[58] Since then, other thinking styles have been identified that are associated with anxiety and personality disorders. These unhelpful thinking styles generate many of the distressing automatic thoughts that support your personality disorder and make your life more difficult.

In many ways these thinking styles are like mind traps, because you continually get caught in them. Periodically, we all fall into these traps, despite the fact that the thought might not be 100 percent accurate. However, people with personality disorders fall into these traps a lot because it has become their habit to do so.

The Eleven Mind Traps

The following is a list of eleven unhelpful thinking styles that people with personality disorders get trapped in.[36, 58] Do your best to identify the ones you use. And despite the examples that are specified for each mind trap, you could be struggling with any of these styles of thinking, no matter which personality disorder you're struggling with. Many of these styles are similar to each other, but don't worry about distinguishing between them. What's important is that you learn to recognize when you're caught in one of these mind traps, so that you can learn how to get out of it.

1. **Filtering**: You make your conclusions after focusing on the negative details of a situation and filtering out all of the positive details. As a result, you don't see the whole picture or you just choose to ignore it. For example, a person who has paranoid personality disorder might think, "Everyone is out to get me," despite the fact that coworkers or family members often offer their support.

2. **Jumping to Conclusions**: You draw negative conclusions despite having no evidence to support them or having evidence that actually contradicts those conclusions. For example, a man who has schizotypal personality disorder might think, "My landlord is going to kick me out of my apartment," despite the fact that the man always pays his rent on time and the landlord hasn't said anything to suggest this.

3. **Overgeneralizing**: You focus on the negative outcomes of one or more limited situations and use those outcomes to make broad, general rules or conclusions about many aspects of your life. People who overgeneralize often use broad, absolute terms, like: every, all, always, none, never, everybody, and nobody. For example, a woman who has avoidant personality disorder might think, "My best friend didn't call me tonight because I must have offended her in some way; now I'll probably offend all of my family members too, and then everybody will hate me," despite the fact that her friend just forgot to call.

4. **Magnifying and Minimizing**: When thinking about yourself, others, or a specific situation, you magnify the negative qualities or minimize the positive qualities. For example, a

person who has narcissistic personality disorder might think, "My coworkers are complete imbeciles who never do anything right," despite the fact that her coworkers are skilled, successful employees.

5. **Personalizing**: This is the tendency to relate everything that is happening around you to yourself, especially negative events that you take the blame for, even when they're not your fault. For example, a man who struggles with histrionic personality disorder might think, "Those people sitting across from me are laughing; I must have done something to embarrass myself," despite the fact that the people across the way aren't paying any attention to him at all.

6. **Black-and-White Thinking**: You see only two categories for people and situations; they are either all good or all bad, perfect or defective, a total success or a complete failure. You neglect looking for compromise or other possibilities. For example, a woman who struggles with borderline personality might think, "My friends are the absolute best and never do anything wrong" or "My friends are the worst and they're always treating me meanly," despite the fact that no one is perfect and we all make mistakes sometimes.

7. **Catastrophizing**: You think that your future will be hopeless and full of catastrophes, without considering other possible outcomes. For example, a person struggling with dependent personality disorder might think, "I can never do anything right by myself, and because of that I'll probably die alone; helpless and homeless, in the streets," despite the fact that the person is sometimes successful at doing things alone and has a number of supportive friends.

8. **Mind Reading**: You assume you know what other people are thinking and feeling, without considering other possibilities. For example, someone with an antisocial personality disorder might think, "My boss doesn't look happy today; I bet he's thinking about the mistake I made last week on my time sheet," despite the fact that his boss could be unhappy due to a completely unrelated person or event.

9. **Rule Making ("Shoulds" and "Musts")**: You have a particular, fixed idea about how things "should" be, and you get upset or angry when your expectations aren't met. For example, a person struggling with obsessive-compulsive personality disorder might think, "I should work harder, because I should never make any mistakes; if I do make a mistake, it must mean I'm a failure," despite the fact that everyone makes mistakes occasionally and nothing is ever perfect.

10. **Emotional Thinking**: You believe that your feelings are judgments about who you are or the situation you're in. For example, a woman who has schizoid personality disorder might think, "I feel lonely, which means I'm probably not a good person," despite the fact that she doesn't feel lonely all of the time and she actually has a few friends.

11. **Labeling**: You attach a negative label or judgment to yourself, others, or your experiences, without looking at all of the facts. For example, a man with an unspecified personality disorder might think, "I'm an idiot," or "My job sucks," despite the fact that these statements are not 100 percent true all of the time.

EXERCISE: Identify Your Own Unhelpful Thinking Styles

What unhelpful thinking styles or mind traps do you use? Record them in the space below:

_____

_____

_____

_____

_____

CHALLENGE YOUR UNHELPFUL THINKING STYLE

Now that you're familiar with some of the most common mind traps, you might be wondering "So what?" And you're right. Just noticing the way you think doesn't help if you don't do something to change it. Depending on which type of mind trap you fall into, you can try using some of the suggestions below to get yourself out of it.

Remember, one of the defining symptoms of a personality disorder is a rigid, inflexible style of thinking. So if you want to improve your life and stop suffering, you need to try thinking in a different way. You need to take a leap of faith, and use some of the alternative responses that are listed below. And learning this one skill isn't going to be enough to change your entire life, but when used in conjunction with many of the other skills you'll learn in this workbook, it just might.

Develop Alternative Responses to Unhelpful Thoughts

If you already recognize the unhelpful thinking style that you use, find it below and learn how you can challenge it. However, if you haven't already identified the style you frequently use, be patient. For the moment, just review the list and become familiar with the unhelpful thinking styles and their alternative responses. Then in the next exercise you'll use this list to explore some new ideas.

1. **Filtering versus Expanding Your Focus**: When you use filtering, you look only at the negative details of a situation and you filter out all of the positive details. Instead, try expanding your focus. Ask yourself, "What am I missing?" or "What am I not looking at?" If you're focusing only on what's going wrong, ask yourself, "What's going well?" or "What's happening that I agree with?" Are you focusing on the problem instead of a possible solution? What might that solution be? For example, if you were thinking, "Everyone is out to get

me," as an alternative, look for evidence of people trying to help you or of your safety right now. Maybe there is some evidence that people are trying to help you and you're choosing to ignore it.

2. **Jumping to Conclusions versus Sticking to the Facts**: When you jump to conclusions, you make negative assumptions despite having no supportive evidence or actually having evidence that contradicts your assumptions. Instead, try focusing on the facts of the situation. Ask yourself two questions: "What facts do I have that my conclusion is accurate?" and "What facts do I have that my conclusion is not accurate?" Then compare the facts, to see if your assumption is correct. For example, if you were thinking, "My landlord is going to kick me out of my apartment," as an alternative, look at the facts. If you pay your rent on time and have a valid lease, your landlord probably can't kick you out, even if he wanted to. Do your best to stay focused on the facts rather than get carried away by your imagination.

3. **Overgeneralizing versus Being Specific**: When you overgeneralize, you focus on the negative outcomes of one or more limited situations and use those outcomes to make broad, general rules or conclusions about many aspects of your life. Instead, be specific about what's really happening. Ask yourself, "Is this situation really as bad as I think? Is it really going to negatively affect any other area of my life?" For example, if you were thinking, "My best friend didn't call me tonight because I must have offended her in some way; now I'll probably offend all of my family members too, and then everybody will hate me," as an alternative, be specific about what happened. There are many possible reasons that could explain the situation and a single bad event doesn't mean that your entire life is ruined. Also, do your best to avoid using broad, absolute terms like "every," "all," "always," "everybody," and so on. Instead, be specific. Even if you did offend one person that doesn't mean that everybody will hate you.

4. **Magnifying and Minimizing versus Thinking in Perspective**: When you magnify and minimize, you enlarge the negative qualities of a situation and minimize the positive qualities. Instead, think about the situation from a new perspective. When you use words like "never," "always," "forever," "complete," and "absolute," you cut yourself off from other possibilities. Similarly, when you use strong negative words to describe people or events, you're only focusing on a single aspect and you lose sight of the whole picture. For example, if you were thinking, "My coworkers are complete imbeciles who never do anything right," as an alternative, ask yourself if your opinion is 100 percent accurate. Maybe your coworkers occasionally make mistakes, but it also is probably true that they're good people who do some things right some of the time.

5. **Personalizing versus Balancing Responsibility**: When you use personalizing, you take the blame for the bad things that happen, even when they're not your fault. Instead, take a look at who is really responsible and do your best to balance the responsibility. Ask yourself, "Am I really 100 percent responsible for this? And if not, who should share the blame?" Maybe you are partly responsible for what's happening around you, but maybe there are other people who are at least partly responsible too. For example, if you were thinking, "Those people sitting across from me are laughing. I must have done something to embarrass myself,

and they're probably laughing at me." As an alternative, ask yourself if you're really responsible for their amusement. Maybe they're laughing at someone else, maybe one of them just told a joke or something else that's completely unrelated to you.

6. **Black-and-White Thinking versus Seeing Shades of Gray**: When you use black-and-white thinking, you see only two categories for people and situations; they are either all good or all bad, perfect or defective, a smashing success or an abject failure. Instead, look at the situation as a shade of gray, in between black and white. Most people are not 100 percent good or bad; we all have our faults. Similarly, most objects have at least small defects, and most events are some combination of success and failure. There are no absolutes in the world. For example, if you were thinking, "My friends are the worst and they're always treating me meanly," as an alternative, try to remember the times when your friends treated you well or, at least, treated you better than they do now. Again, look for evidence that balances or contradicts your judgments.

7. **Catastrophizing versus Considering All Your Possibilities**: When you catastrophize, you think that your future looks hopeless and full of disasters, without considering any other possible outcomes. You're one hundred percent certain that the worst-case scenario will occur. Instead, consider the possibility that the worst disaster *won't* happen. Ask yourself, "If the worst-case scenario doesn't occur, what else might happen?" Be fair in your assessment. Be creative; consider even the most remote possibilities. For example, if you were thinking, "I can never do anything right by myself, and because of that I'll probably die alone, helpless and homeless, in the streets," as an alternative, consider what else might happen. You might learn how to help yourself by using the skills in this workbook, you might get help from your family, or you may end up living in a nice home with a loving family. Chances are that something better is just as likely to happen as the catastrophe you're worried about. So why not hope for the best?

8. **Mind Reading versus Asking for Clarification**: When you mind read, you assume that another person is thinking something negative about you, without considering any other possibilities. Mind reading is one of those things that we all do sometimes, which just makes us feel worse about ourselves. However, you can't really know what other people are thinking unless they tell you. So if you want to know, go ahead and ask the person what he or she is thinking in a calm, polite way. For example, if you were thinking, "My boss doesn't look happy today; I bet he's thinking about the mistake I made last week on my time sheet," as an alternative, ask your boss what's wrong. You could say, "I noticed you look upset, may I ask what's bothering you?" If the other person does have a problem related to you, asking for clarification will give you and that person an opportunity to work it out. However, don't be surprised if the other person wasn't thinking about you at all. Remember, your assumptions aren't always true.

9. **Rule Making versus Being Flexible**: When you engage in rule making, you have a particular, fixed idea about how things should be, and you get upset or angry when your expectations aren't met. Instead, be flexible in how you judge yourself and others. And remember, your rules and values aren't shared by everyone, so don't judge them if you wouldn't want

them to judge you. Instead, ask yourself, "How can I be flexible in this situation so that everyone can be somewhat happier or more satisfied? How can I make a fair compromise?" For example, if you were thinking, "I should work harder because I should never make any mistakes; if I do make a mistake it must mean I'm a failure," as an alternative, ask yourself if that's a fair and flexible statement. Everyone makes mistakes and the only thing that making a mistake really means is that you're human, just like the rest of us.

10. **Emotional Thinking versus Rational Thinking**: When you use emotional thinking, you believe that your feelings are true judgments about who you are or the situation you're in. Instead, use rational thinking and look at the evidence to determine whether your judgments are 100 percent true. Emotions can be wonderful, but they're just temporary electrical and chemical signals within your body. They aren't permanent and they aren't always accurate descriptions of who we are or what kind of situation we're in. For example, if you were thinking, "I feel lonely, which means I'm probably not a good person," as an alternative, look at the evidence. Ask yourself, "What good things do I do sometimes? Is it possible that I'm feeling lonely and I'm a good person at the same time?" Most likely it is.

11. **Labeling versus Remaining Nonjudgmental**: When you label, you attach a negative label or judgment to yourself, others, or your experiences without looking at all the facts. Instead, do your best to remain nonjudgmental of yourself, others, and the situation. Whenever you use an insulting term to describe yourself, you cut yourself off from other possibilities; if you're "dumb," there are many things you can't do. Similarly, when you label and judge others and situations you automatically place negative expectations on them. Instead, leave yourself open to all possibilities. For example, if you were thinking, "I'm an idiot," as an alternative, create a nonjudgmental coping statement that helps you through your problem, such as "I don't feel good, but I'll do the best I can." Similarly, if you were thinking, "My job sucks," create a coping statement like "I'm not happy with my job right now, but I've gotten through rough times in the past." Nonjudgmental statements like this make it possible for you to engage in new behaviors.

Unhelpful Thinking Styles and Alternative Responses

Unhelpful Thinking Styles	Alternative Responses
These are the mind traps that you use, which generate unhelpful, automatic thoughts.	These are the new, healthier responses you can try whenever you find yourself caught in one of the unhealthy thinking styles or mind traps.
1. **Filtering:** You make conclusions after focusing on the negative details and filtering out all of the positive details.	1. **Expanding Your Focus:** Ask yourself, "What am I not looking at?" If you're focusing only on what's going wrong, ask yourself, "What's going well?" or "What's happening that I agree with?"
2. **Jumping to Conclusions:** You draw negative conclusions, despite having no evidence to support them or having evidence that actually contradicts those conclusions.	2. **Sticking to the Facts:** Ask yourself, "What facts do I have that my conclusion is accurate?" and "What facts do I have that my conclusion is not accurate?" Then compare the facts to see if your assumption is correct.
3. **Overgeneralizing:** You focus on the negative outcomes of one or more limited situations and use those outcomes to make broad, general rules or conclusions about many aspects of your life.	3. **Being Specific:** Ask yourself, "What are the facts of this situation? Is it really as bad as I think? Is it really going to negatively affect any other area of my life?" Also, avoid using broad, absolute terms, like: every, all, always, none, never, everybody, and nobody.
4. **Magnifying and Minimizing:** When thinking about yourself, others, or a situation, you magnify the negative qualities or minimize the positive qualities.	4. **Thinking in Perspective:** Ask yourself, "Is my opinion 100 percent accurate? What are some other aspects of this situation that I'm not looking at?"
5. **Personalizing:** When something bad happens, you take the blame for it, even when it's not your fault.	5. **Balancing Responsibility:** Ask yourself, "Am I really 100 percent responsible for this? If not, who should share the responsibility? Who else is at least partly responsible?"
6. **Black-and-White Thinking:** You see only two categories for people and situations; they are either all good or all bad, perfect or defective, a success or a failure.	6. **Seeing in Shades of Gray:** Ask yourself, "Am I being fair? Is anything really 100 percent good or bad? What possibilities am I missing when I choose to see things in black-and-white terms?"
7. **Catastrophizing:** You think that your future will be hopeless and full of catastrophes, without considering other possible outcomes.	7. **Considering All Your Possibilities:** Ask yourself, "What else might happen? What possibilities am I not considering? Can my situation improve in any way?"
8. **Mind Reading:** You assume you know what other people are thinking and feeling, without considering other possibilities.	8. **Asking for Clarification:** Ask yourself, "Can I really know what anyone else is thinking, without the person telling me?" Obviously you can't. So if you want clarification, go ahead and ask the person or stop guessing altogether.
9. **Rule Making:** You have a particular, fixed idea about how things "should" be, and you get upset or angry when your expectations aren't met.	9. **Being Flexible:** Ask yourself, "How can I be flexible in this situation so that everyone can be somewhat happy or satisfied? How can I make a fair compromise?"
10. **Emotional Thinking:** You believe that your feelings are true judgments about who you are.	10. **Rational Thinking:** Ask yourself, "What's the evidence that my judgments are 100 percent true? Is there another explanation for the way I'm feeling?"
11. **Labeling:** You attach a negative label or judgment to yourself, others, or your experiences, without looking at all the facts.	11. **Remaining Nonjudgmental:** Ask yourself, "Am I being fair to myself, others, and the situation? What possibilities am I cutting myself off from?"

Create Alternatives to Your Unhelpful Thinking Styles

Now that you're familiar with the common, unhelpful thinking styles and their alternatives, let's put this skill into action. To begin, read the following example:

Patrick struggled with paranoid personality disorder. When he filled out his Thought Journal, he recognized that he often had thoughts like, "I can't trust anyone," "People are trying to harm me," and "Others don't deserve my forgiveness." But after reading about unhelpful thinking styles and alternative ways of thinking, he was able to challenge some of those thoughts and to think of alternative ways to respond to his thoughts. Take a look at his example below of using the worksheet called Challenge Your Unhelpful Thinking Styles.

Observe that Patrick was able to come up with a number of healthier thoughts by first identifying the unhelpful thinking styles he was using and then choosing to use appropriate, alternative responses. But more importantly, notice that after challenging his thoughts, he rerated his emotions and found some relief, which is the best reason to challenge your automatic thoughts. Remember, your thoughts and feelings influence each other. So if you learn how to change your thoughts, you can also soothe your emotional experiences.

EXERCISE: Challenge Your Unhelpful Thinking Styles

Use the Challenge Your Unhelpful Thinking Styles worksheet below to challenge some of the automatic thoughts you recorded in your Thought Journal. Do your best to identify the unhelpful thinking styles that you were using and then try to create healthier alternative responses. And remember, the purpose of this exercise is not to make you an expert at identifying the unhelpful thinking styles by name. The purpose is to help you learn to think in a healthier, more flexible way. So even if you can't identify your specific unhelpful thinking style, still do your best to create an alternative thought. And if that thought generates some new type of behavior, as in Patrick's example ("Some people said hello, maybe I could trying saying hello to them."), try doing the new behavior (saying hello to others) and see what happens.

For the next three to four weeks, continue to record your automatic thoughts on this new worksheet and do your best to create healthier, alternative responses.

Challenge Your Unhelpful Thinking Styles–Patrick's example

Situation	Feelings	Automatic Thoughts	Unhelpful Thinking Style	Alternative Thought or Response	Rerate Feelings
When did the situation occur? Where were you? Who was involved? What happened?	Describe your feelings during the situation and rate their intensities from 0 to 10 (0 = no intensity, 10 = greatest intensity).	What were you thinking before you noticed the unpleasant feeling? Or what were you thinking during the emotional experience?	Identify the mind trap you fell into: Filtering, Overgeneralizing, Personalizing, etc.	Challenge your unhelpful thinking style using an alternative thought or response.	After considering alternatives, rerate your feelings from 0 to 10 intensity.
On train to work	Anxious (8)	"I can't trust anyone."	Magnifying	Thinking in Perspective: "I can trust a few people, like my family and closest friends."	Anxious (5)
Walking to work	Scared (7)	"People are trying to harm me."	Filtering	Expanding Your Focus: "Some people said hello, maybe I could trying saying hello to them."	Scared (3)
Walking home from work	Angry (8)	"I often feel threatened by others."	Emotional Thinking	Rational Thinking: "Maybe I felt angry because of something else, not because people were threatening me."	Angry (4)
Having dinner with Carl	Worried (6)	"People will betray me if given the chance."	Jumping to Conclusions	Sticking to the Facts: "Carl hasn't done anything to hurt me and I was having a nice dinner with him."	Worried (3)
Talking to my brother	Upset (7)	"Others don't deserve my forgiveness (if they don't do what I tell them to do)."	Rule Making	Being Flexible: "My brother does the best he can, although he doesn't always listen to me. I could try to support him."	Upset (5)

Challenge Your Unhelpful Thinking Styles–Patrick's example

Situation When did the situation occur? Where were you? Who was involved? What happened?	Feelings Describe your feelings during the situation and rate their intensities from 0 to 10 (0 = no intensity, 10 = greatest intensity).	Automatic Thoughts What were you thinking before you noticed the unpleasant feeling? Or what were you thinking during the emotional experience?	Unhelpful Thinking Style Identify the mind trap you fell into: Filtering, Overgeneralizing, Personalizing, etc.	Alternative Thought or Response Challenge your unhelpful thinking style using an alternative thought or response.	Rerate Feelings After considering alternatives, rerate your feelings from 0 to 10 intensity.

CHALLENGE YOUR THOUGHTS BY EXAMINING YOUR PAST EXPERIENCES

So far in this chapter you've learned how to:

- Identify your automatic thoughts

- Identify unhelpful thinking styles that promote those thoughts

- Challenge those unhelpful styles with alternative thoughts

Ideally, you've given yourself at least six to eight weeks to practice these skills and hopefully you've experienced some emotional relief. However, if you're still having trouble challenging some of your automatic thoughts, the following technique might be helpful. In this section, you'll learn how to examine your past experiences to find evidence that both strengthens and weakens the validity of your automatic thought. Then you'll create a more balanced, alternative thought using that information. This skill is very helpful, especially if your automatic thought is preventing you from taking some kind of action. This technique is largely based on the work of psychologists Dennis Greenberger and Christine Padesky in their book *Mind Over Mood*.[59]

Identify Past Experiences That Strengthen the Validity of Your Automatic Thought

This first step is usually the easiest. Most people who struggle with self-critical automatic thoughts can often think of several experiences from their past that support or strengthen the validity of those thoughts. For example, Scarlett struggled with schizoid personality disorder and had great difficulty socializing with other people. One day at work, some of her colleagues asked her to go bowling with them, but the thought of spending time with them made her feel scared, embarrassed, and worried. First, she worked through this difficult situation using the Challenge Your Unhelpful Thinking Styles worksheet, but she still needed help because she couldn't decide what to do. So her next step was to examine her most troublesome automatic thought by searching for experiences that both strengthened and weakened its validity. The thought that bothered her the most was "I'll be very awkward in that situation, so I shouldn't go." When she thought about past experiences that strengthened the validity of her automatic thought she came up with three examples very easily:

1. Whenever I go out with other people, I never know what to say to them.

2. I don't know how to bowl and I always embarrass myself.

3. The last time I went out with a friend I didn't have a good time.

EXERCISE: Record Experiences That Strengthen Your Automatic Thought

This is your chance to act like a defense lawyer during a trial. First identify your troublesome automatic thought and describe how it makes you feel. Then, pretend you've been asked to provide the facts that strengthen your belief in your automatic thought. Do your best to remember all of the past experiences that support your assumption that your thought is true.

My automatic thought is: _____

This thought makes me feel: _____

The past experiences that strengthen my automatic thought are: _____

_____

_____

_____

_____

_____

_____

_____

_____

_____

_____

_____

Identify Past Experiences That Weaken the Validity of Your Automatic Thought

This second step is usually harder than the first one. The goal here is to look for past experiences that weaken or contradict the validity of your automatic thought. Often it's helpful to ask yourself some of the following questions:

1. Have you had any similar past experiences that turned out better than you thought they would? Scarlett noted, "I've gone out with colleagues before and it's been okay."

2. Are you exaggerating the overall accuracy of your automatic thought? For example, is it true that the situation will lead to the outcome that you've predicted or are there other possibilities? Scarlett wrote, "Sometimes I act pleasantly in those social situations."

3. Are there any exceptions to the conclusions that you've drawn? Scarlett noted, "Lately, I've been talking with a few coworkers without much fear."

4. Are there other factors that might reduce the negativity of the automatic thought or the feared situation? Scarlett wrote, "In the past, it has felt good to go out sometimes, even when it has been difficult for me."

5. If you were to look at this situation realistically or from someone else's perspective, what's most likely to happen? Scarlett said, "Most likely, nothing very bad will happen. I might just feel uncomfortable like I have in the past."

6. What could you do to cope with the situation in a new, more effective way? For example, are there certain skills or techniques that you could use? Scarlett noted, "I could excuse myself and leave if I feel too nervous, like I've done in the past."

7. Do you know someone who could help you or can you think of someone who would handle this situation in a more effective way? If so, what would that person do? Scarlett wrote, "I'll ask [my friend] Ann to stay close by. She's been a good friend to me."

EXERCISE: Record Experiences That Weaken Your Automatic Thought

Once again, pretend that you're a lawyer building a big case. But this time you're on the other side and your job is to find information and experiences that weaken the validity of your automatic thought.

The past experiences that weaken my automatic thought are: _____

_____

_____

_____

_____

_____

_____

_____

_____

_____

_____

_____

Create an Alternate, Balanced Thought

After you've found experiences that both strengthen and weaken your automatic thought, it's very important to create an alternate, balanced thought—which you believe—and identify how that new thought makes you feel. Read over the experiences you recorded in the two previous exercises and try to put them together in a way that is both fair and balanced. It might be as easy as joining a thought from both exercises, but whatever you do, make sure that your new thought is one you truly believe, not just a thought that you've created for the sake of finishing the exercise. When you're done, do your best to identify any new actions you can take and how the new thought makes you feel. Notice if the emotion is different than the original one you recorded, even if it has lessened just a little in intensity.

In Scarlett's example, she was able to create the following balanced thought, "I might feel very awkward going out with people from work, but this is something that I'm working on and in the past I've been able to get along in some social situations. Plus, it might be good for me to get out and I might even enjoy myself a little." She was also able to identify a new plan of action based on this thought: "I'll go out with my colleagues and do the best I can." Plus, she recognized that she felt less scared, embarrassed, and worried, and even a little hopeful.

EXERCISE: Create an Alternate, Balanced Thought

Based on the experiences you discovered that both strengthen and weaken the validity of your automatic thought, do your best to create an alternate, balanced thought that is more accurate. Also, identify what new actions you will take and how you feel.

My alternate, balanced thought is: _____

_____

_____

_____

My new plan of action is: _____

_____

_____

_____

Based on my new thought and plan of action I now feel: _____

_____

_____

IN CONCLUSION

Hopefully, you've had some success using the skills in this chapter to:

1. Identify your automatic thoughts

2. Challenge the ones that are causing you distress

3. Improve the way you feel

However, these goals will be met only if you take the time to complete the Challenge Your Unhelpful Thinking Styles worksheet on a consistent basis and examine your past experiences, if necessary. With regular practice, you'll start to notice some changes. First, you'll notice that you're filling out the worksheets more willingly. Next you'll notice that you can complete them more easily. And, lastly, you'll start to think of alternate, balanced thoughts more automatically, without having to use the worksheet.

Before you move on to the next chapter, be sure to spend at least six to eight weeks challenging your automatic thoughts. While you do, search for similar thoughts that keep showing up. These will be helpful in the next chapter. Also, remember to continue scheduling both pleasant and mastery activities into your daily life using the Weekly Activity Schedule.

CHAPTER 6

Challenge Your Negative Core Beliefs

While you were identifying and challenging your automatic thoughts using the Challenge Your Unhelpful Thinking Styles worksheet over the last six to eight weeks, you might have noticed that some of your distressing thoughts kept repeating or were very similar to each other in their subject matter. These commonalities often point to core beliefs. Core beliefs are deep, strongly held thoughts you have about yourself, others, the world, or your future.[58] These thoughts act as the blueprints for your life, and they frequently influence your behavior, your emotions, and your relationships.

Core beliefs can be either positive or negative in quality. Positive core beliefs like "I can do anything that I set my mind to" allow you to tackle challenges and help you to get through difficult times. But negative core beliefs like "I'm a failure" can make you less likely to succeed, interfere with your relationships, and leave you more vulnerable to feelings of frustration, loneliness, and sadness. Common negative core beliefs also include thoughts like "I'm defective," "I'm worthless," and "I'm unlovable."

Most negative core beliefs develop early in childhood.[36] Some children are told directly by their parents and friends that they aren't good enough or smart enough, while other children are treated in ways that makes them feel unlovable or defective. In addition, some children learn their core beliefs by watching the way people—especially their parents—interact with others. However, no matter how your own core beliefs began, over time you started believing that those negative beliefs about you were true, even if they really weren't. Then over time, these negative core beliefs began to influence how you thought, felt, and behaved in the world.

THE GOALS OF THIS CHAPTER

Core beliefs are powerful, and changing them might sound difficult, but it's not impossible. Developing healthier core beliefs is the most important skill you'll learn in this workbook and it deserves your time and effort, even when the work becomes challenging. Overall, the goals of this chapter are to help you:

1. Identify your negative core beliefs

2. Identify the rules and predictions of your negative core beliefs

3. Test the rules of your negative core beliefs

4. Create new, healthier core beliefs

Much of the theory and many of the exercises in this chapter are based on the work of mental health experts like Aaron Beck and Arthur Freeman,[36] Jeffrey Young,[60] and Matthew McKay and Patrick Fanning.[61]

STEP 1: IDENTIFY YOUR NEGATIVE CORE BELIEFS

Both positive and negative core beliefs establish the rules by which you live your life. Most often you're probably not even aware that you're thinking about your core beliefs or using them as rules to live by. They've become such a part of your personality that you simply believe "This is who I am and that's how I do things." But hopefully, by this point in the book, you've already seen proof that you can change your thoughts and create new, healthier experiences.

Later, we'll look at creating new, positive core beliefs, but for now, let's focus on identifying your negative core beliefs and seeing how they affect your life. In essence, negative core beliefs filter your experience and cause you to focus on certain types of distressing experiences and emotions while ignoring other, more pleasant experiences and emotions. For example, a man who has the negative core belief "I'm defective" might think that he is incapable of doing anything correctly, even if he has had successes in the past. For that reason, it's likely that (1) he'll dismiss his past successes and say they're insignificant; (2) he won't take risks; (3) he'll rely on others for constant reassurance; and (4) he'll usually associate with people who confirm his feelings of being defective.

Similarly, a woman with the negative core belief "I'm unlovable" might believe that she'll be lonely and disappointed for her whole life, even if she has had some healthy relationships in the past. As a result, she might do the following: (1) she'll regard the few healthy relationships she had in her past as either being out of the ordinary or take no credit for having formed them; (2) she'll stop trying to meet new people and going on dates; (3) she'll stop taking care of herself and stop trying to improve her life; and (4) she'll continually become involved with others who make her feel unlovable, such as with people who abuse her or take advantage of her.

It might sound strange that the people in both of these examples take actions that reinforce their negative core beliefs instead of behaving in ways that change those beliefs, but more often than not, this is what happens. Too often, negative core beliefs such as these greatly influence people's lives, even when those beliefs lead to suffering.

To help you identify your own negative core beliefs there are two techniques that you can use: theme analysis and the downward arrow technique. Both of these techniques will require you to look deep within yourself and to examine how you are living your life. This can be difficult. Negative core beliefs are always attached to powerful emotions, and when you identify yours, you should expect to feel some degree of sadness, fear, or regret. But don't be discouraged; with some dedicated work, you can change these negative beliefs as well as these negative emotions.

Theme Analysis

As mentioned at the beginning of this chapter, when you were filling out your Challenge Your Unhelpful Thinking Styles worksheet over the past several weeks, you might have observed that certain repetitious thoughts kept coming up or several problematic situations appeared to be very similar. Perhaps you'll recognize that many of your distressing thoughts share the same general theme, such as "I always fail," "People are always trying to hurt me," "I can't do anything for myself," or "I'll always be alone." Or maybe you recognize that you feel distressed whenever you are in social situations. Looking at both your problematic thoughts and situations can help you to uncover your negative core beliefs.

For example, when Hillary, who struggled with histrionic personality disorder, reviewed her lists of automatic thoughts, she found that many of her thoughts focused on attracting attention from other people, expressing her belief that she wasn't good enough, and her feelings of loneliness. After reviewing her lists of automatic thoughts, she summarized them with this statement of a negative core belief: "Unless other people are paying attention to me, I never feel good enough." She knew she was on the right track because this thought made her feel sad. It also sounded very familiar, as if she had thought it many times.

EXERCISE: Sum Up Your Automatic Thoughts in a Single Statement

Right now, go back and review your Thought Journal and Challenge Your Unhelpful Thinking Styles worksheet and record any of your common themes or thoughts below. Then try to sum up these thoughts in a single statement.

_____

_____

_____

_____

_____

Downward Arrow Technique

Another way of identifying your negative core beliefs is to use a technique called the downward arrow. This technique tries to drill below the thoughts that you normally are aware of, to uncover the hidden negative beliefs that may lie beneath many of your habitual automatic thoughts.

From your lists of automatic thoughts, find one about yourself that you frequently think. Then ask yourself, "If that thought is true, what does it mean about me?" Next, take your answer and ask, "If that's also true, what does *that* mean about me?" And keep going in a similar manner. Keep asking yourself the same question; that is, "If that thought is true, what does it mean about me?" until you can go no further. But more importantly, keep going until you find an answer that arouses a strong emotional response. At that point, you'll know you've found something important about yourself that deserves to be examined and challenged.

For example, Vivian struggled with personality disorder not otherwise specified. She recognized that one of her common automatic thoughts was "Other people should take care of me." Then she asked herself, "If that's true, what does it mean about me?" Her answer was "I need other people's help." She then asked, "If that's also true, what does that mean about me?" Her response was "I always need lots of people around who are willing to do things for me." She continued, "So if that's true, what does it mean about me?" Eventually, Vivian arrived at an answer that made her feel extremely sad, so she knew that she had identified her negative core belief, which was "It means there's something wrong with me and that I'm not able to take care of myself."

If Vivian had diagrammed her thoughts using downward arrows, they would have looked like this:

"Other people should take care of me."

↓

"I need other people's help."

↓

"I always need lots of people around who are willing to do things for me."

↓

...

"It means there's something wrong with me and that I'm not able to take care of myself."
(This is Vivian's negative core belief.)

EXERCISE: Using the Downward Arrow Technique

When completing this exercise, be sure to respond to the question "If that's true, what does that mean about me?" only with thoughts, not with feelings. For example, don't respond to the question with "I feel sad." Instead, identify the thought or belief that makes you feel sad.

Use the downward arrow technique below to uncover your negative core belief. Start by recording one of your common automatic thoughts, and continue until you arrive at your negative core belief.

First, write down your frequent automatic thought:

_____

_____

↓

If that thought is true, what does it mean about you?

_____

_____

↓

And if that thought is true, what does it mean about you?

_____

_____

↓

And if that thought is true, what does it mean about you?

_____

_____

↓

Continue for as long as necessary:

_____

_____

_____

_____

Common Negative Core Beliefs of Personality Disorders

According to many cognitive behavioral therapists, people with similar personality disorders often share similar negative core beliefs. Now that you've attempted to identify your own negative core beliefs, check the list of examples below. Perhaps they will help you to clarify the core belief that you're struggling to identify. However, it's important to remember that these examples are just generalizations and that your particular negative core belief might be very different.

According to psychiatrist Aaron Beck and his associates, people with personality disorders often struggle with negative core beliefs like these:[36]

- **Antisocial personality disorder:** "I have to take care of myself because no one else will," "I'm entitled to get what I want no matter what the rules say," and "Other people will take advantage of me unless I take advantage of them first."

- **Avoidant personality disorder:** "I'm defective," "I'm unlovable," and "There's something wrong with me, so it's best to stay away from other people so they won't discover my faults."

- **Borderline personality disorder:** "I'm defective (or worthless)," "Other people will hurt me," and "I can't ever be alone, so I need to do whatever it takes to make others stay with me."

- **Dependent personality disorder:** "I'm completely incapable of doing anything by myself," "If I'm ever alone, I'll die," and "I'm completely helpless, so I'll always need someone to assist me."

- **Histrionic personality disorder:** "I'm not valuable (or lovable) unless other people are admiring me," "I'm worthless without other people's attention," "I need to entertain people (or be interesting enough) for them to like me."

- **Narcissistic personality disorder:** "I'm more important than other people and I deserve special privileges," "Society's rules don't apply to me the way they do to ordinary people," and "If other people don't treat me as special, then they deserve to be punished."

- **Obsessive-compulsive personality disorder:** "I'll fail unless I maintain very high standards for myself and for everyone else," "I should do everything perfectly," "I must maintain control of all the details, otherwise I'll be overwhelmed (or things will fall apart)," and "Everything has to be done perfectly, so I have to be in control of everything to prevent any errors from occurring."

- **Paranoid personality disorder:** "Other people want to hurt me (or take advantage of me)," "I'm vulnerable to being harmed," and "I always have to be on guard to protect myself."

- **Schizoid personality disorder:** "I don't need close relationships because they only interfere with my life," "I'm better off alone," "I'm not capable of forming close relationships," and "I shouldn't get close to other people."

- **Schizotypal personality disorder:** "I don't fit in with other people," "Other people want to hurt me (or take advantage of me)," and "I'm not capable of forming close relationships."

- **Personality disorder not otherwise specified:** "I'm unlovable," "There's something wrong with me," and "I always mess up, so why bother trying?"

EXERCISE: Record Your Own Negative Core Beliefs

Now that you've completed the theme analysis and downward arrow exercises, as well as having reviewed some common negative core beliefs, it's time to record your own negative core belief(s) in the space below. Don't be surprised if you identify several that need to be challenged. Many people struggle with more than one negative core belief, such as "I'm unlovable" and "I need someone to take care of me."

My negative core beliefs include:

_____

_____

_____

_____

_____

_____

===

STEP 2: IDENTIFY THE RULES AND PREDICTIONS OF YOUR NEGATIVE CORE BELIEFS

Now that you've identified one or more of your negative core beliefs, it's time to challenge them and determine whether they're really true or not. Of course, you probably live your life as if these beliefs are true, but have you ever stopped to ask yourself if your beliefs are absolutely true? That is, would most other people agree with you that your beliefs about yourself are true? One way to test the truth of your negative core beliefs is to challenge the rules that support them.

Each core belief carries with it an unspoken set of rules that determines how you live your life, what you're allowed to do and not do, and how you should interact with other people. Unfortunately, the rules of negative core beliefs are very restrictive and often prevent people from living fulfilling lives. For example, a man who holds the belief "I'm unlovable and defective" might live by the following rules: (1) "I should never seek out healthy, loving relationships" (since he's unlovable); and (2) "I should always ask for other people's help before I do anything" (since he can't do anything correctly by himself). Similarly, a woman who has the negative core belief "I'm going to be abandoned by the people I care about" might live by these rules: (1) "I should never disagree with other people" (since they might leave her as a result); and (2) "I should sacrifice my own needs to help others meet their needs" (in order to please other people).

Identify Your Own Rules

Now, let's identify how your own negative core beliefs are interfering with your life. In their book *Prisoners of Belief*[61] Matthew McKay and Patrick Fanning suggest that you can identify your rules by observing how you react to different troubling situations that trigger your core beliefs. First, read through the following list of twenty-one triggering situations, the list of eight questions below the triggering situations, and the examples that are provided. Then in the exercise that follows, answer the questions for yourself on several sheets of blank paper.

List of Triggering Situations

1. Coping with other people's emotions (especially anger, criticism, disappointment, and sadness)

2. Dealing with other people's love and support for you

3. Handling your own emotions

4. Coping with mistakes (yours or those of others)

5. Asking for help or support from others

6. Being alone or with others

7. Trusting others

8. Making friends

9. Having conversations or being social

10. Coping with romantic or sexual relationships

11. Dealing with work or career issues and problems

12. Relating to your family or children

13. Handling success (yours or others')

14. Dealing with stressful or problematic situations

15. Handling new or challenging situations

16. Expressing your own feelings, opinions, or limits

17. Handling your own health issues or someone else's

18. Coping with your spiritual beliefs and activities

19. Engaging in fun and recreational activities

20. Taking care of yourself

21. Taking care of others

Now ask yourself how your negative core belief causes you to behave in each of the triggering situations listed above. Every answer that you come up with is a rule that you follow—for better or for worse. If you need help identifying how you react in each of the triggering situations, answer as many of the following questions as you can for each situation.

1. How does your negative core belief cause you to react in this situation?

2. What do you do to avoid distressing feelings that are caused by your belief and the situation?

3. What do you do to avoid the situation or the people associated with it?

4. What do you do to avoid problems created by the situation instead of dealing with them directly?

5. What do you do to protect yourself in the situation?

6. Do you limit yourself in some way as a result of your belief and the situation?

7. Do you do something that reinforces or confirms your belief about yourself?

8. Do you do anything else in this situation as a result of your belief?

Here's an example of how using the list of triggering situations and answering the questions can help you to discover some of the rules that may govern your life.

Nathan was struggling with narcissistic personality disorder. After working through many Thought Journal and Challenge Your Unhelpful Thinking Styles worksheets, he had realized that he held the following core belief: "I'm undesirable to others." Then he used both the list of triggering situations and the eight questions to uncover the rules of his core belief.

To begin, he took the first situation—coping with other people's emotions—and he answered as many of the questions as he was able to. Here are his responses:

- Answer to question 1: "Because I believe that I'm undesirable to others, I ignore them when they express any emotion whatsoever."

- Answer to question 2: "Because I believe that I'm undesirable to others, when people express emotion it makes me feel anxious and I usually avoid feeling that way by criticizing the other people."

- Answer to question 5: "Because I believe that I'm undesirable to others, when people express emotion I protect myself by acting superior to them."

Then he moved onto the next situation—dealing with other people's love and support—and again he answered as many of the questions as he could. He continued until he had reviewed the entire list of twenty-one triggering situations and had answered as many questions as possible. Here are his responses to the last situation—taking care of others:

- Answer to question 3: "Because I believe that I'm undesirable to others, I avoid taking care of others by not doing anything at all and by not getting close to anyone."

- Answer to question 7: "Because I believe that I'm undesirable to others, I don't take care of anyone, which makes me feel like a selfish jerk, which then makes me feel even more undesirable."

When Nathan finished reviewing the list of triggering situations and had answered as many questions as possible, he realized he had recorded sixty-one answers. Each answer represented an unhealthy rule that he followed as a result of his negative core belief. When Nathan attempted to summarize all of his rules he discovered that four of them were very dominant in his life: (1) "I find it very difficult—if not impossible—to ask anyone for help"; (2) "When other people express emotions, I ignore them or belittle them"; (3) "I never volunteer for challenging situations at work"; and (4) "I never help others."

EXERCISE: Discover Your Own Rules

Now do your best to discover your own rules. On a sheet of paper, record the core belief that you're exploring, as well as the ways you react to the triggering situations as a result of that belief. Use the eight questions if you need help. Be as honest and as specific as you can when you record your answers. If you have trouble recognizing your own rules, go through the list of triggering situations in a slower, more thorough way.

When you've completed the exercise, record the dominant rules you discovered in the space below:

My core negative belief is:

_____

_____

My rules are:

_____

_____

_____

_____

_____

_____

_____

_____

Identify Your Negative Predictions

Now that you've recognized several rules that result from your negative core belief, you can next identify what you think will happen if you don't follow those rules. The consequences that you imagine are probably very powerful negative predictions that prevent you from challenging your rules. Let's continue looking at Nathan's example. Here are his negative predictions based on his core belief and its rules.

Rules and Negative Predictions—Nathan's Example

Core belief: *"I'm undesirable to others."*

1. Rule: *Don't ask anyone for help.*

   Negative prediction: *People will get annoyed with me and then will abandon me.*

2. Rule: *Don't react when others express emotions.*

   Negative prediction: *I'll do something wrong and the person will feel insulted.*

3. Rule: *Don't volunteer for anything difficult at work.*

   Negative prediction: *I'll probably mess it up; I might cause a huge problem, and then I'll be fired.*

4. Rule: *Don't bother helping others.*

   Negative prediction: *If I do something wrong, they'll get angry with me.*

EXERCISE: Identify Your Own Negative Predictions

Now identify the negative predictions that are attached to each of your own rules. Use the space provided below and a blank sheet of paper if necessary. If you have trouble identifying your negative predictions, ask yourself the following questions. If you don't follow your rules:

- What awful event will take place?

- What are you afraid will happen?

- What's the worst that could happen?

- Will someone get hurt?

Rules and Negative Predictions

Core belief: _____

1. Rule: _____

   Negative predictions: _____

   _____

   _____

2. Rule: _____

   Negative predictions: _____

   _____

   _____

3. Rule: _____

   Negative predictions: _____

   _____

   _____

4. Rule: _____

   Negative predictions: _____

   _____

   _____

5. Rule: _____

   Negative predictions: _____

   _____

   _____

STEP 3: TEST THE RULES OF YOUR NEGATIVE CORE BELIEFS

This third step in the process of challenging your core beliefs is often the hardest for many people. In order to challenge your negative core beliefs, you must test your rules and your negative predictions to see whether they're true or not. Often this means doing the exact opposite of what the rule requires or finding another way to challenge the rule. By doing this, you'll generally find that although your negative predictions may sound very powerful, in truth they are usually inaccurate.

For example, one of Nathan's rules was "Don't ask anyone for help" because his negative prediction said, "People will get annoyed with me and then abandon me." He decided to test this rule by asking some neighbors to help him move some furniture in his apartment. To his surprise, he discovered that his neighbors were happy to help him and that no one got annoyed. Clearly, his prediction was very inaccurate. This not only caused Nathan to question the accuracy of his rule, but it also changed the way he thought about himself and others. He had learned that people were sometimes happy and more than willing to help him.

How to Test Your Rules

Testing the rules of your core belief will take some courage. For a very long time you've strengthened your rules by following them. Now you're being asked to break them. Generally, this requires you to do the exact opposite of what the rule says to do, to see if your negative predictions come true. For this reason, you need to make a commitment to yourself to test your rules in a specific way. Throughout the process, follow these guidelines:

1. **To begin, test a rule that's fairly low on a difficulty or fear scale.** On a scale of 0 to 10, with 10 being extremely difficult or frightening, start by picking a rule that's a 2 or a 3.

Then, as you gain confidence with early successes, you can start challenging harder rules that feel more intimidating.

2. **Pick a rule that's easy to set up in a situation that you can initiate.** For example, it was far more effective for Nathan to create a situation in which he could ask his neighbors for help, rather than waiting for a random situation to occur when he might ask a stranger for help.

3. **Make a plan to test your rule.** When are you going to test it? Where? What are you going to do? What might get in the way of testing your rule, and what could you do about that? For example, Nathan knew that his neighbors were usually home on Saturday around noon, so he planned to do it then. And if his neighbors weren't at home, he knew that he could try again the following day around the same time.

4. **Create a situation in which you can observe immediate outcomes.** For example, if Nathan decided to test his rule of expressing his opinions to someone else, it would be more effective to do so when he was with other people rather than expressing his thoughts in a letter or an e-mail, because he would then have to wait for the person's response.

5. **Test your rule in such a way that you can observe other people's behavioral responses.** You want to be able to see if your negative predictions come true. You don't want to rely on reading someone else's mind or guessing about other people's feelings to determine their responses. For example, Nathan volunteered to do a small project at work, which he completed and gave to his supervisor. But rather than guess at his supervisor's reactions, Nathan went to her office so he could directly observe her responses, which were positive.

6. **Prepare to test your rule.** There are many strategies you can use. You can write down what you're going to say or do in the situation, much like creating a movie script. Then you can use an audio or video device to record what you plan to say and how you will say it. This will allow you to determine if your words, tone of voice, and body language are appropriate for the situation. You can also practice what you plan to do in front of a mirror, or you can rehearse the situation with someone you trust, much like rehearsing a scene for a play. Another way to prepare is to use your imagination. That is, you can visualize the details of the situation and imagine yourself completing the test successfully.

7. **Record the outcome of your test.** Did it go better or worse than you feared? Did your negative prediction take place, or did something else happen? Did something get in the way of testing your rule? If things went differently than you thought they would, why do you think they went differently? Was the rule as difficult to test as you thought it would be? And, most importantly, what did you learn from this experience? Be as specific as possible about what happened as a result of your test. Even if something trivial occurred, it might help you build a body of evidence that contradicts your negative core belief. And remember, you should be engaging in tests where you can observe how the test affects other people (if others are involved); so if you're not sure how it affected them, then ask. Say something like, "Was it okay with you that I asked you to do that?" or "Was it okay with you that I did that?" Do your best to get honest feedback about your actions, rather than trying to guess about their effectiveness.

If challenging the rules of your core belief still feels too intimidating, use a stress-reduction technique from chapter 7, like progressive muscle relaxation or mindful breathing, to help you relax both before and after you challenge the rule. In addition, you can consult chapter 10, Learn Coping Imagery, or chapter 11, Use Exposure to Confront Feared Situations and Emotions, to learn additional techniques that will help you test your rules.

Use the following Test Your Rules worksheet to challenge the rules of your negative core beliefs. (Make additional photocopies as needed.) After you successfully challenge less intimidating rules, begin challenging more difficult ones. And most importantly, remember to record your progress and save the forms that you complete. Many people fail to write down the results of their tests, and so they forget their successes.

Over the course of the next several weeks or months, do your best to challenge as many of your rules as possible. Do this before moving on to Step 4: Create New, Healthier Core Beliefs. While you are challenging your rules, continue to schedule pleasurable and mastery activities into your life.

Test Your Rules

BEFORE TESTING

Negative core belief: _____

Rule of the belief: _____

_____

Negative predictions: _____

_____

How will you test the rule? _____

_____

Will there be immediate observable results? _____ (If your answer is no, revise your plan.)

When will you test the rule? _____

Where? _____

What might get in your way, and what could you do about it? _____

_____

How can you prepare? _____

Predicted difficulty rating (0–10): _____

AFTER TESTING

What happened? _____

_____

Did your negative predictions come true? _____

_____

What did you observe? _____

_____

If things went differently, why? _____

_____

Actual difficulty rating (0–10): _____

What did you learn from this experience? _____

_____

STEP 4: CREATE NEW, HEALTHIER CORE BELIEFS

Now that you've had several weeks or months to challenge the rules of your negative core beliefs, you've probably encountered some successes. Hopefully you've had new, unexpected experiences that contradict your rules and negative predictions. It's likely that you now realize your worst fears don't always come true, despite how intimidating or scary they might have seemed to you.

Perhaps you've also started to think about yourself, others, and the world in a different, healthier, more balanced way. For example, if your original core belief was "I'm unlovable," maybe now you think, "Sometimes I still feel unlovable, but I often have experiences with others when I know they like me or even love me." Or if your core belief was "I'm defective," maybe now you think, "Sure, sometimes I don't do things perfectly; nevertheless, I often do a very good job." Do you see the difference? It's subtle, but it's important. Your negative core beliefs aren't going to change permanently overnight. In fact, you might continue to think about yourself in your old way from time to time for the rest of your life, but hopefully testing your rules has helped you develop the psychological flexibility to think about yourself in a healthier, more positive way sometimes.

Now that you've tested your old rules, it's time to reprogram the way you think about yourself, your future, and others, so that you can start living according to positive core beliefs and new, healthier rules. The exercises below will help you to develop a new positive core belief and a related set of rules. Then, after you've had some success developing one positive belief, you should consider working through this process again to develop additional positive core beliefs for yourself.

State Your New Belief

To begin, you first need to state a healthier, positive core belief about yourself and the way you want to interact with other people. Usually, this positive core belief will come from the work you've done testing your old rules. For example, Dwight, who has dependent personality disorder, had the negative core belief "I'm completely incapable of doing anything by myself." However, after testing the rules of this belief, he realized that he was capable of completing many tasks successfully without the constant support of others. As a result of his tests' positive outcomes, he rewrote his positive core belief as, "I'm a capable person who can do many things without the help of others." Similarly, Hillary, who has histrionic personality disorder, had the negative core belief "I'm worthless without other people's attention." When she tested her rules, she discovered that other people liked her even when she wasn't the center of attention. As a result, she created a new core belief that said, "I'm a likable, worthy person who doesn't have to try so hard."

WHAT IS YOUR NEW CORE BELIEF?

Based on the work of testing your old rules that you've completed, record the new core belief you'd like to have about yourself, even if you don't believe it completely right now:

_____

_____

_____

State Your New Rules

Next, you need to create the new set of rules that you intend to live by, based on your new, positive core belief. But instead of creating rigid "If...then" rules (that is, if someone does this, then I'll do that), consider developing rules that highlight your overall positive qualities and reinforce your positive core belief. A good test for your new rule is to ask yourself whether it's fair to both you and the people you interact with. For example, based on her new core belief that said, "I'm a likable, worthy person who doesn't have to try so hard," Hillary developed the following new rules: (1) "I can relax, even when I feel anxious"; (2) "I'll do my best to be friendly, but it's still okay if I'm not liked by everyone"; and (3) "I can be quiet and reserved sometimes and people will still want to be my friends."

WRITE YOUR NEW RULES

When you first write down these new rules for yourself, don't be surprised if they sound very strange, as if someone else had written them. You shouldn't expect that these new rules will magically feel comfortable or that they will automatically be easy to set in motion. These new rules will be challenging but, hopefully, you're willing to experiment with them and to test the hypothesis that they will improve your life.

Based on your new, positive core belief, record at least three new rules you intend to follow:

1. _____

2. _____

3. _____

Record Your Progress with New Belief and Rules

Now that you've created a healthier core belief and a new set of rules to live by, it's time to put them into action and record your progress. You should look for frequent opportunities every day to test your new belief and rules, and then you should record the evidence of your progress. Remember, these rules aren't going to change quickly; it's going to take an honest effort on your part to change your life. This process might take months or even years, but it's certainly worth the effort to achieve a happier, healthier life and better, happier relationships with other people.

Use the following Positive Core Belief Evidence Log to record your new beliefs, your new rules, and the experiences that reinforce them. Be sure to record what happened during the new experience and what you learned about yourself and others. Do your best to add at least one experience to the form every day. Either keep a copy of the form with you to record experiences as they happen, or make a point of recording at least one event before going to sleep each night.

As you begin testing your new rules, keep in mind that some situations may be easier than others. You might need to start testing your new rules in less intimidating situations before you test them in more challenging situations later, just as you did when you tested your old rules. And again, if you need additional help, use a stress-reduction technique from chapter 7, like progressive muscle relaxation or mindful breathing, or consult chapter 10, Learn Coping Imagery, or chapter 11, Use Exposure to Confront Feared Situations and Emotions, to learn additional techniques that will help you test your new rules.

Positive Core Belief Evidence Log

Original negative core belief: _____

_____

New positive core belief: _____

_____

1. New positive rule: _____

   _____

   - How did you test the new rule? _____

     _____

   - What happened? _____

     _____

   - What did you learn from this experience? _____

     _____

     _____

2. New positive rule: _____

   _____

   - How did you test the new rule? _____

     _____

   - What happened? _____

     _____

   - What did you learn from this experience? _____

     _____

     _____

Examples of Using the Positive Core Belief Evidence Log

Refer to the following examples of positive core beliefs and rules that are provided below for each of the personality disorders. But remember, these are just examples, and your own new beliefs and rules may be very different.

ANTHONY: ANTISOCIAL PERSONALITY DISORDER

- Original negative core belief: "Other people will take advantage of me unless I take advantage of them first."

- New positive core belief: "People are generally nice to me if I try to be nice to them."

- New positive rule: "I'll help someone at work every day."

  - How did you test the new rule? "I helped Tanya put the heavy water bottle into the watercooler."

  - What happened? "She thanked me."

  - What did you learn from this experience? "I don't have to keep my guard up all the time. I can be nice to people sometimes and they'll appreciate it."

AVA: AVOIDANT PERSONALITY DISORDER

- Original negative core belief: "I'm defective."

- New positive core belief: "I might not be an expert at everything, but I do lots of things well enough."

- New positive rule: "I'll take on new challenges whenever possible."

  - How did you test the new rule? "I sorted through the stack of mail that has been sitting on my desk for the last two months."

  - What happened? "It was difficult, but I got through it and now it's done."

  - What did you learn from this experience? "I'm stronger than I often think I am."

BRITNEY: BORDERLINE PERSONALITY DISORDER

- Original negative core belief: "I can't ever be alone, so I need to do whatever it takes to make others stay with me."

- New positive core belief: "I'm a strong, confident woman who is capable of being alone sometimes."

- New positive rule: "When opportunities arise to be alone, I'll welcome them."

  - How did you test the new rule? "I stayed home on Saturday night and read a book."

- What happened? "I enjoyed the book and my time by myself. It was very peaceful."

- What did you learn from this experience? **"Sometimes I actually enjoy being alone, and I can cope with it."

DWIGHT: DEPENDENT PERSONALITY DISORDER

- Original negative core belief: "I'm completely incapable of doing anything by myself."

- New positive core belief: "I'm a capable person who can do many things without the help of others."

- New positive rule: "I'll look for opportunities to complete tasks by myself."

  - How did you test the new rule? "I volunteered for a project at work and asked to do it alone."

  - What happened? "I completed the project and my manager gave me some feedback about how I could improve my performance next time, although he was generally satisfied with what I did."

  - What did you learn from this experience? "I'm sometimes more skilled than I think I am."

HILLARY: HISTRIONIC PERSONALITY DISORDER

- Original negative core belief: "I'm worthless without other people's attention."

- New positive core belief: "I'm a likable, worthy person who doesn't have to try so hard."

- New positive rule: "I can be quiet and reserved sometimes and people will still want to be my friends."

  - How did you test the new rule? "I went out with friends from work and behaved modestly, without showing off."

  - What happened? "Friends and colleagues came over to talk to me anyway."

  - What did you learn from this experience? "I don't need to be the center of attention in order to connect with my peers."

NATHAN: NARCISSISTIC PERSONALITY DISORDER

- Original negative core belief: "I'm more important than other people and I deserve special privileges."

- New positive core belief: "I can play by the same rules as everyone else and still get my own needs met."

- New positive rule: "I'll ask for what I need rather than demand that other people just give it to me."

  - How did you test the new rule? "I asked my coworker Beth if she could help me organize a luncheon (rather than giving her an order to do so)."

  - What happened? "She looked surprised. Then she said she was busy at the moment and would talk to me about it later. When she did, she said she'd be happy to help."

  - What did you learn from this experience? "I don't have to give orders to get what I want. I can act like other people and still get my needs met."

OLIVIA: OBSESSIVE-COMPULSIVE PERSONALITY DISORDER

- Original negative core belief: "I should do everything perfectly."

- New positive core belief: "I don't have to do everything perfectly; I'll still keep my job and maintain my family."

- New positive rule: "I'll leave work on time, even if my tasks aren't completed."

  - How did you test the new rule? "I left work at 5 p.m. and went home to have dinner with my family."

  - What happened? "My boss didn't reprimand me, and my family was happy to have me home for dinner."

  - What did you learn from this experience? "I can satisfy my boss, my family, and myself."

PATRICK: PARANOID PERSONALITY DISORDER

- Original negative core belief: "I always have to be on guard to protect myself."

- New positive core belief: "I can be safe and still let my guard down sometimes."

- New positive rule: "I will let my guard down around the people I know."

  - How did you test the new rule? "I went to a family party and told them about what I'd been doing lately."

  - What happened? "Nothing. No one tried to take advantage of me or use the information to harm me."

  - What did you learn from this experience? "It's safe to be around certain members of my family."

SCARLETT: SCHIZOID PERSONALITY DISORDER

- Original negative core belief: "I'm not capable of forming close relationships."

- New positive core belief: "Maybe I lack relationship experience, but I can still try to form friendships with people."

- New positive rule: "I'll make opportunities to form new relationships whenever possible."

  - How did you test the new rule? "I went to lunch with some colleagues from work."

  - What happened? "We chatted about our lives and gossiped about what was happening in the office. My colleagues were very friendly and said I should come out with them more often."

  - What did you learn from this experience? "I don't have to form perfect friendships immediately. My colleagues were patient and friendly."

SCOTT: SCHIZOTYPAL PERSONALITY DISORDER

- Original negative core belief: "I don't fit in with other people."

- New positive core belief: "I don't fit in with everybody, but there are lots of people with whom I do fit in."

- New positive rule: "I'm going to find groups of people with whom I share common interests."

  - How did you test the new rule? "I went to a party and looked for people who were wearing interesting clothes and tried talking to them."

  - What happened? "Some of them said they felt awkward at parties too. One of them invited me to a get-together at her house next weekend."

  - What did you learn from this experience? "Other people often feel out of place, too. I'm not the only one. I can connect with others pretty easily."

VIVIAN: PERSONALITY DISORDER NOT OTHERWISE SPECIFIED

- Original negative core belief: "I always mess up, so why bother trying?"

- New positive core belief: "I sometimes do things successfully, and no one is perfect."

- New positive rule: "I'll challenge myself with tasks, even when I'm not sure that I'll succeed."

  - How did you test the new rule? "I offered to help my son paint a room in his house, even though I've never done that before."

  - What happened? "He said my painting looked like it was done by a professional."

  - What did you learn from this experience? "I'm capable of handling challenges, including things I've never done before.

IN CONCLUSION

Hopefully, this chapter has showed you how to challenge your negative core beliefs and helped you develop new positive core beliefs. As you continue to work on these skills, remember to be patient with yourself and with the process. Most people with personality disorders have been struggling with their negative core beliefs for many years, so these habits of thought will take a good amount of time and effort to modify. But remember, developing positive core beliefs is definitely the most important skill you will learn in this workbook. So keep working hard to create them and your new rules as you continue to develop the other skills that are explained in the following chapters.

CHAPTER 7

Practice Stress-Reduction and Relaxation Techniques

Remember the following diagram from chapter 5? It shows how your thoughts, feelings, and behaviors all interact and influence each other:

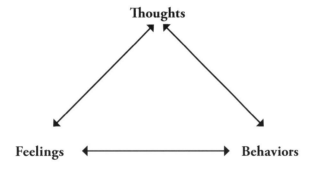

So far, the previous chapters have shown you how to think and behave in healthier, more helpful ways. In this chapter, you'll learn how to soothe both your physical and emotional feelings using a variety of stress-reduction and relaxation techniques.

WHY THESE TECHNIQUES ARE IMPORTANT

For most people, changing the habits associated with their personality disorders is very challenging, and therefore the process can cause both physical and mental strain. Stress-reduction and relaxation techniques can help to reverse some of these effects, and they can also help you to confront those challenges in a more successful way.

Let's look at an example. Ava struggled with avoidant personality disorder. She regularly avoided dealing with big problems, and she also avoided making common, everyday decisions, like what to have for dinner. As a result, many of her relationships became strained, and she frequently suffered with mental anxiety and physical symptoms of stress, such as tight muscles and headaches. Ava achieved great success when she challenged her distressing thoughts and engaged in new activities using a Weekly Activity Schedule, but she also realized that she needed additional help to soothe her body and mind. So she started using many of the relaxation techniques you will find in this chapter—especially before engaging in an activity that she'd been avoiding—and soon she recognized that it was easier to make tough decisions and confront stressful situations when she felt more relaxed.

GOALS OF THIS CHAPTER

Like Ava, you may find making changes in your life difficult. Often, your own anxious thoughts and stressful physical sensations make matters worse. For this reason, stress-reduction and relaxation techniques are very important when you are in the process of changing the habits associated with your personality disorder. As you read this chapter, practice all of the techniques discussed and then choose the ones that work best for you. Then, as you continue the work of challenging your behavioral and cognitive habits, you can use these techniques when you:

- Feel physical or mental strain

- Plan a difficult task in your Weekly Activity Schedule

- Challenge your distressing thoughts

- Restructure your core beliefs

- Engage in other techniques that change your habits, such as problem solving, coping imagery, and stress inoculation.

But, remember, each of these skills requires practice in order to be effective. Mastering some techniques might require a few days, and others might need several weeks. Don't give up. Remember, you've spent many years making yourself feel anxious and tense; now you'll need an adequate amount of time to practice feeling relaxed.

Many of the exercises described in this chapter were adapted from *The Relaxation and Stress Reduction Workbook*[62] and *The Dialectical Behavior Therapy Skills Workbook*,[63] and you should consult those books to learn additional similar skills.

THE BODY SCAN EXERCISE

Typically, relaxation exercises begin with building body awareness. This exercise will help you learn how to scan your body for signs of muscle tension so that you can learn to release that tension and to relax. This exercise should take only about ten or fifteen minutes. Practice the body scan exercise at least once a day for one week before trying the next exercise, which is called progressive muscle relaxation.

Read the instructions before beginning the exercise in order to become familiar with the process. Then you can refer to them again or you can record the instructions and listen to them while observing the sensations in your body.

Don't be surprised if your focus begins to wander while you're doing this exercise. When you recognize that your attention is drifting, gently return your focus to the exercise, and do your best not to criticize or judge yourself.

EXERCISE: The Body Scan

To begin, find a comfortable place to sit in a room where you won't be disturbed for at least ten minutes. Turn off any distracting sounds. Take a few slow, long breaths, and then close your eyes. When you begin the exercise, observe any sensations you notice in your body, especially muscle tension. For now, don't try to release the tension. Just do your best to notice it, continue to breathe, and try to stay focused on the activity. Make sure to spend enough time on each section of your body to notice all of the sensations there, before you move on to the next area of your body.

First, focus on your feet. Notice any sensations in your toes, the soles of your feet, your ankles, and the tops of your feet. You might notice tingling or tension. For now, just notice it and continue to breathe. (Pause here.)

Now notice your lower legs, including your calf muscles, shins, and knees. Observe any sensations there and continue to breathe. (Pause here.)

Next focus on your upper legs and your hamstrings, thigh muscles, buttocks, and genital area. Notice the weight of your body supported by the chair you're sitting in. Notice any other sensations and continue to breathe. (Pause here.)

Then notice the front of your torso, including your stomach and chest area. Observe any sensations and continue to breathe. (Pause here.)

Now notice your lower and upper back. Pay attention to any muscular sensations or tension as you scan this area. Notice any other sensations and continue to breathe. (Pause here.)

Next focus on your shoulders, upper arms, and elbows. Observe any sensations there and continue to breathe. (Pause here.)

Then notice any sensations in your forearms, hands, and fingers. Slowly scan both the tops and bottoms of your hands. Observe any sensations there and continue to breathe. (Pause here.)

Now focus on the front and back of your neck. Observe any sensations there and continue to breathe. (Pause here.)

Next notice any sensations in your face, especially around your jaw, mouth, nose, eyes, and forehead. Notice any signs of tension there, including a tight jaw and forehead. Observe any other sensations in your face and continue to breathe.

And, finally, notice any sensation around the rest of your head, especially near your ears and the top of your skull. Observe any other sensations there and continue to breathe. (Pause here.)

When you've finished the exercise, open your eyes and take another minute to sit quietly before returning your focus to the room.

PROGRESSIVE MUSCLE RELAXATION

Hopefully, you've been practicing the body scan exercise and now feel comfortable locating and observing the tension in your body. Progressive muscle relaxation is the next step in helping you learn to release muscle tension, reduce anxiety, and relax. This exercise is based on the work of physician Edmund Jacobson. In his book *Progressive Relaxation*, Jacobson observed that anxiety frequently caused muscle tension, and therefore, if you can learn to release that tension, you can also soothe your feelings of anxiety.[64]

In a safe and systematic way, progressive muscle relaxation will guide you through tensing and relaxing different muscle groups throughout your whole body. As you do this, pay attention to the feeling of relaxation that occurs after you release the tension. If you experience any pain while doing these exercises, stop immediately. In addition, if you already are experiencing any chronic pain issues, such as arthritis, back pain, or joint pain, consult your medical professional before conducting this exercise. Otherwise, proceed with caution. You can gently tense any of these muscle groups without experiencing pain and still benefit from the exercise.

Remember, the purpose of this exercise is not to tense your muscles to the point of exertion or strain; it is to help you identify what relaxed muscles feel like in comparison to tight muscles. Many people habitually tense their muscles, especially in the neck and shoulder area, without noticing it. Over time, these habits can lead to chronic back pain, shoulder pain, and headaches. The goal of progressive muscle relaxation is to help you notice any muscle tension that you're carrying and quickly release it, and by doing so, hopefully you'll relieve some anxiety as well.

As with all of the exercises in this book, the more you practice progressive muscle relaxation, the faster you will experience its benefits. It's recommended that you practice this skill at least once a day for a few weeks, or twice a day if you frequently feel tense or anxious. While doing this exercise you might find it easier to wear loose, comfortable clothing that allows you to bend and stretch. Also, when you release the tension from each group of muscles, you might obtain additional benefit by using a suggestive word or phrase to help you relax, like "Peace," "Relax," or "Let go of the tension." And, lastly, when releasing your muscle tension, do your best to release it quickly and completely, rather than slowly. This will help to emphasize the difference between the tight feeling and the relaxed feeling.

Read through the exercise before beginning. Then you can either refer to the script again, or you can record the instructions and listen to them while observing the sensations in your body.

EXERCISE: Progressive Muscle Relaxation

To begin, find a comfortable place to sit in a room where you won't be disturbed for fifteen minutes. Turn off any distracting sounds or lights. Take a few slow, long breaths, and then close your eyes. As you breathe, remember that the point of this exercise is to notice the difference between muscle tension and muscle relaxation. Don't overstrain your muscles during this exercise. Tighten each muscle group only until you feel a gentle tension, and then release it. This is especially important when you're tightening and releasing your feet, back, and neck muscles. If you experience any pain during the exercise, stop immediately.

When you're ready to begin, gently inhale and hold your breath while you curl your toes under, on both feet. Notice how the muscle tension feels. Hold the tension for approximately five seconds. (Count, "One, two, three, four, five.") Then exhale while you quickly and completely release the tension in your feet. (If you want to use a helpful word like "relax," say it each time when you release the tension.) Now notice the released feeling in your toes and feet. Notice how different it feels. Then, again gently curl your toes under, without exerting too much pressure on them, while you inhale and hold your breath. Notice how the muscle tension feels. Hold the tension for five seconds, and then quickly and completely release it while you exhale. Again, notice the released feeling in your toes and feet and note how different it feels compared to the tense feeling.

Next gently inhale and hold your breath while straightening your legs and pointing the toes of both of your feet. Notice the tension in your legs and feet. Hold your breath and the tension for approximately five seconds. Then exhale and release the tension quickly. Notice the sensation in your muscles as the tension is released. Feel the relaxed sensation in your muscles and notice how different it feels from the tensed feeling. Then, when you're ready, repeat this exercise for this muscle group one more time.

Now gently inhale and hold your breath while you bend your arms at the elbows and tighten both of your hands into fists—like a bodybuilder posing. Notice the tension in your upper arms, forearms, hands, and fingers. Hold your breath and the tension for five seconds. Then exhale and release the tension quickly. Notice the sensation in your muscles as the tension is released. Feel the relaxed sensation in your muscles and notice how different it feels from the tensed feeling. Then, when you're ready, repeat this exercise for this muscle group one more time.

Next gently inhale and hold your breath while you tighten your stomach and chest muscles. Imagine that you're hugging a large beach ball as you bend forward and curl around it. Notice the tension in your stomach, chest, and back. Hold your breath and the tension for five seconds. Then exhale and release the tension quickly as you sit up straight. Notice the sensation in your muscles as the tension is released. Feel the relaxed sensation in your muscles and notice how different it feels from the tensed feeling. Then, when you're ready, repeat this exercise for this muscle group one more time.

Now gently inhale and hold your breath while you straighten your arms with your fingers pointing toward the ground and raise up your shoulders toward your ears. Notice the tension in your upper back, neck, and shoulders. Hold your breath and the tension for five seconds. Then exhale and release the tension quickly. Let your shoulders drop. Notice the sensation in your muscles as the tension is released. Feel the relaxed sensation in your muscles and notice how different it feels from the tensed feeling. Then, when you're ready, repeat this exercise for this muscle group one more time.

Finally, gently inhale and hold your breath while you tighten the muscles of your face. Tighten the muscles around your mouth, eyes, and forehead and notice the tension. Hold your breath and the tension for approximately five seconds. Then exhale and release the tension quickly. Notice the sensation in your facial muscles as the tension is released. Feel the relaxed sensation in your muscles and notice how different it feels from the tensed feeling. Then, when you're ready, repeat this exercise for this muscle group one more time.

When you've finished the exercise, take another minute to sit quietly before returning your focus to the room in which you are sitting.

RELEASE-ONLY RELAXATION

After you've had success practicing progressive muscle relaxation, try releasing your tension by mentally focusing on each group of muscles. Do not tense up your muscles first; just let them release. Use the same order of muscles as you did in the last exercise (for example, first your feet, then your legs, and so forth). But this time, just use your memory of what your muscles feel like when they're relaxed to let go of any tension. Each time you notice tension, do your best to let your muscles release, lengthen, and let go. Breathe normally throughout this exercise without holding your breath. Or if it's helpful, imagine releasing your muscle tension each time you exhale. Spend as much time as you need focusing on each group of muscles and releasing any tension you find. With daily practice, this technique can help you relax your whole body in just a few minutes.

EXERCISE: Cue-Controlled Relaxation

A cue is a signal that reminds you to do something. This technique will teach you to relax by using a word or phrase to remind yourself to do so.

To begin, use the release-only relaxation technique to help you fully relax. Take a few minutes. Then, after you're feeling peaceful, shift your focus to your breath. As you inhale, think of the words "Breathe in," and as you exhale, use a word or phrase like "Relax," "Peace," or "Let go," as you might have done with progressive muscle relaxation. Continue to breathe and use your cue word to create a deeper sense of relaxation: "Breathe in…" then "Relax…" Practice this technique once or twice a day for at least two weeks (and be sure to remember to use the release-only technique first).

After you've had several sessions of successful practice, see if you can induce a state of relaxation just by thinking of your cue word. For an added challenge, try doing this before you do something difficult, like talking to someone you've been avoiding or trying something new.

MINDFULNESS SKILLS

Mindfulness is the ability to be aware of your thoughts, feelings, and actions in the present moment. Have you ever heard the expression "Be in the moment"? This is another way of saying, "Be mindful of what's happening to you right now." Developing your mindfulness skills is one of the most important things you can do to overcome your personality disorder. By definition, people struggling with personality disorders are stuck in rigid patterns of thinking and behaving that interfere with their lives. In order to get out of that pattern, you first have to become aware of what it is you're doing. Awareness is the first step for changing anything. You need to start asking yourself, "What's happening right now? What am I thinking?

What am I doing? What's the other person doing? How am I reacting to it all?" Then, after you've become aware of what's happening, you can begin reacting in newer, healthier, and less stressful ways.

Let's look at an example. Britney struggled with borderline personality disorder. Part of her problem was making quick, critical judgments about herself and others, which then led to upset feelings and anger. One day at work, Britney saw her friend Joan across the room but Joan didn't see her, so Joan left the room. Very quickly, Britney had these thoughts: "She's ignoring me. Why doesn't she like me anymore?" Then Britney started to feel very hurt and angry. To deal with her anger and to relieve the stress she felt, she went to the ladies' room and began chewing her fingernails until her cuticles were bleeding.

In this example, Britney's reactions were so quick and unmindful that she reacted automatically without being aware of what was happening. If she'd been more mindful of what she was thinking and she'd challenged some of her thoughts, the situation might have developed like this: "She's ignoring me. Why doesn't she like me anymore? Wait. That's a very negative thought. Maybe she's not ignoring me. Maybe Joan just didn't see me. Or maybe she's in a bad mood today. Joan has been a good friend to me. I'll check with her later."

If Britney had been more mindful of her emotions, she might have done the mindful breathing exercise (see below) to help herself relax after she felt angry. If she had been more mindful of her actions, she might have gone somewhere private to do some progressive muscle relaxation to release the tension from her body instead of hurting herself.

Mindful Breathing

Mindful breathing is an important skill that uses long, slow breaths—in through the nose and out through the mouth—to help you relax and focus your concentration. This is a very important skill, especially for people who frequently feel anxious or stressed out. When you feel anxious, it's natural to breathe more quickly and more shallowly. Unfortunately, this style of breathing naturally increases your feelings of anxiety. To counteract this, you'll need to learn how to do mindful breathing.

This type of breathing activates the diaphragm muscle at the bottom of your lungs and helps you take slower, longer breaths, and as a result, it naturally helps you feel more relaxed and focused. To recognize whether you're properly using your diaphragm muscle, place one hand on your stomach as you breathe. If you're breathing correctly, you should feel your stomach gently rise as you inhale, as if you were filling a balloon with air. Then as you exhale, you should feel your stomach gently fall, as if the balloon were deflating.

Note that some people find it difficult to breathe this way because their abdominal muscles are generally tight and releasing them to breathe is difficult. When people are anxious or stressed, they naturally tense their abdominal muscles, which causes them to take short, shallow breaths using the muscles of their upper chest and shoulders. This can easily be detected by placing one hand on your stomach and the other hand on your upper chest as you inhale. Ideally, you should feel little movement under the hand resting on your chest. If you do feel greater movement there and little movement in the abdominal muscles of your stomach, you'll need to practice releasing your abdominal muscles as you breathe. Again, imagine your stomach as a balloon that gently inflates while you inhale and gently deflates while you exhale.

When first practicing this form of breathing, some people find it easier to lie down, rather than sit in a chair. Lying down often makes it easier to notice the rising and falling of your stomach. If this is true for you, feel free to begin your practice this way. Eventually, however, you should transition to practicing in a seated position since this is the position in which most people spend much of their time, such as while driving or at work. Then later on, you can even practice while standing and walking.

Ideally, mindful breathing should be performed by breathing in through your nose and out through your mouth. However, some people might find it difficult to breathe in through their nose. If this is true for you, feel free to inhale through your mouth, but do so slowly, as if you were breathing in through a straw, rather than taking quick gulps of air.

Be aware that some people might become light-headed or experience tingling in their lips or fingertips when practicing mindful breathing. This usually means that you're breathing too fast or too deeply. If you experience any symptoms like this, stop doing the exercise and return your breathing to its normal state. Then, when you're feeling better, try breathing more slowly and less deeply.

EXERCISE: Mindful Breathing

Read through the script below before beginning, to familiarize yourself with the process. Again, if you'd like to listen to them while you are doing the exercise, you can record the instructions. Then set a kitchen timer or an alarm clock for five minutes and practice breathing until the alarm goes off. (As you become more accustomed to this technique, you can set the alarm for longer periods of time, such as for ten or fifteen minutes.)

To begin, find a comfortable place to sit or lie down in a room where you won't be disturbed. Turn off any distracting sounds. Place one hand on your stomach. Now slowly breathe in through your nose, and then slowly exhale through your mouth, as if you were slowly blowing out birthday candles. Feel your stomach rise and fall as you breathe. Imagine your belly gently filling up with air like a balloon as you breathe in, and then feel it gently deflate as you breathe out. Focus on your breath moving in through your nose and out through your mouth in a slow, gentle rhythm. (Pause here.)

As you breathe, notice the sensations in your body. Feel your lungs gently fill with air. Notice your stomach rising and falling. Notice the weight of your body being supported by whatever you're sitting or lying on. With each breath, notice how your body feels more and more relaxed. (Pause here.)

Now, as you continue, focus your concentration on your rate of breathing. For example, as you inhale, feel the air moving in through your nose and say to yourself, "Inhale." As you exhale, feel the air moving past your lips and say to yourself, "Exhale." (Or try silently counting your breaths each time you exhale. Count each exhalation until you reach four, and then begin counting at one again.) (Pause here.)

Do your best to stay focused on your breathing. When your mind wanders and you catch yourself thinking of something else, gently return your focus to your breathing. Think, "Inhale," or start counting from one to four again. Try not to criticize yourself for getting distracted. (Pause here.)

Continue taking slow breaths in through your nose and out through your mouth. Feel your stomach filling up with air like a balloon. Notice as it gently rises and falls. Stay focused on each breath, and with each exhale feel your body relaxing. Keep breathing until your alarm goes off, and then slowly return your focus to the room.

EXERCISE: What's Happening Now?

Here's a mindfulness exercise that sounds easier than it really is. The goal is to check in with yourself throughout the day, in order to remind yourself to be mindful.

Throughout the day, simply ask yourself, "What's happening now?" Maybe you'll be driving, so say to yourself, "Now I'm driving." Perhaps you'll notice that your foot hurts, so say to yourself, "Now I'm noticing my foot hurts." Maybe you'll recognize that you're thinking about something, so simply note, "Now I'm thinking about..." Or perhaps you'll just be aware of the sounds around you, so note, "Now I'm hearing..." Keep your observations short, and begin them with "Now I'm..." Again, the goal is to become more aware of what you're thinking, feeling, and doing in the present moment so that you can change any unhelpful habits that are contributing to your personality disorder.

Asking yourself, "What's happening now?" might sound like a fairly simple exercise to do, but the hardest part is remembering to do it. Leave reminders around your home, car, and office to prompt yourself. Use a sticky note with a message on it, like "Now?" The more you practice, the more automatic the process will become and the easier it will be to catch yourself having unmindful thoughts and making unmindful actions.

Daily Mindfulness

Do your best to incorporate mindfulness exercises into all of your daily activities. The more you do them, the easier they will become. Here are two examples.

EXERCISE: Mindful Walking

Try doing a walking meditation. Walk slowly in an area where you won't be disturbed. Notice the feel of the ground beneath your feet. Notice how the pressure changes on your feet and toes as you shift your weight and move. Notice what's around you. Notice the sounds you hear. Start with a walk of a few minutes and, as it gets easier, increase the time or distance.

EXERCISE: Mindful Eating

Another exercise is to try mindful eating. Use a small piece of food, such as a nut, a small candy, or a fruit. Begin by holding it in your hand. Notice how it feels, how much it weighs, the color, the shape, and any other details. Then put the piece of food into your mouth and, without chewing, notice how it feels and tastes on your tongue. Then slowly start chewing and swallowing the food while staying aware of the entire process.

Be Mindful of Your Judgments

In chapter 5, you practiced recognizing and challenging your distressing automatic thoughts. Judgments—critical statements about yourself and others—are a type of automatic thought that takes you away from the present moment and often leads to distressing feelings. Whenever you make a judgment about something or someone (including yourself), you get distracted from the present moment and get caught in a dialogue inside your own head. Plus, even if your judgment is somewhat truthful, it can still trigger distressing feelings like sadness, anger, and anxiety.

Here's an example. Dwight, who has dependent personality disorder, was in a meeting in which his boss was discussing upcoming projects. As his boss was talking, Dwight began judging himself. "I hope he doesn't pick me for a project. I'm such an idiot; I wouldn't be able to do it without someone else's help." His own thoughts made him feel very anxious and scared. Then to make matters worse, while Dwight was busy judging himself, his boss asked him a question that he didn't hear and couldn't answer.

If Dwight had been aware of his initial judgmental thought—"I'm such an idiot"—perhaps he could have responded with a thought like the one you learned in the exercise What's Happening Now? "Now I'm judging and I need to return my focus to what's happening." Then he would have returned to the present moment and heard his boss's question, and more importantly, he would have felt much less anxious.

Sometimes stopping a thought is difficult or nearly impossible, but in most cases you can detach yourself from it. Instead of getting caught up in your thought the way Dwight did, you notice that you're making a judgment, and then you let go of it so you can return your focus to the present moment. This is difficult and it takes practice, but with time your judgments will become less troublesome.

EXERCISE: Judgment Record

To help yourself detach from your critical thoughts, try keeping a Judgment Record. Do your best to write down your judgmental thoughts as soon as they happen or at least once a day. Then, when you're making a judgment, use a statement like one of the following to detach from your judgment and return to the present moment:

- "Now I'm judging."
- "Stop."
- "Let go of the judgment."
- "Go back to the present moment."

With practice, you'll start to recognize more of the judgments as you're making them, and as a result, you'll be able to disconnect from them and return to what's happening in the present moment. Doing so should relieve some of your distressing feelings. Make as many photocopies of the following blank Judgment Record as you need, or simply re-create the worksheet on a blank piece of paper.

JUDGMENT RECORD

What was the judgment?	How did it make you feel? (Do your best to describe it.)	What did you do or say to return to the present moment?	How did you feel after returning to the present moment?

SAFE-PLACE VISUALIZATION

Safe-place visualization is a powerful stress-reduction technique. When using it, you can soothe yourself by imagining a peaceful, safe place where you can relax. Often, your brain and body can't tell the difference between what's really happening and what you're just imagining. So if you can successfully create a peaceful, relaxing scene in your thoughts, your body will often respond to those soothing ideas.

EXERCISE: Safe-Place Visualization

Make sure you conduct this exercise in a place where you'll be free from distractions. Read through the script below before you begin and, if you like, record them so that you can listen while doing the exercise. Before you begin the exercise, think of a real or imaginary place that makes you feel safe and relaxed. It can be a real place that you've visited in the past, such as a beach, a park, and so on. Or it can be a place that you've completely made up, such as a white cloud floating in the sky, a medieval castle, or the surface of the moon. If you have trouble thinking of a place, think of a color that makes you feel relaxed, such as pink or baby blue. Just do your best to choose something that you know is relaxing. In the exercise, you'll be guided to explore this place in greater detail. But before you begin, make sure you already have a safe place in mind.

To begin, sit or lie down in a comfortable place and feel the weight of your body being supported. Close your eyes. Using your mindful breathing skills, take a few slow, long breaths in through your nose and exhale slowly through your mouth. Feel your belly expand and collapse like a balloon, as you breathe in and out. Continue breathing slowly until you start to feel at ease.

Now, with your eyes closed, imagine that you are entering your safe place. First, look around using your imaginary sense of sight. What does this place look like? Notice the details. Are you alone or with other people? If with others, what are they doing? Notice the environment around you. Are you inside or outside? Is it light or dark? Choose something soothing to look at, and if there are details you'd like to change to make the scenery more soothing, change whatever you'd like to change. Take as long as you like to look at the details. (Pause here.)

Next use your imaginary sense of hearing. What do you hear in your scene? Other people? Music? The wind? The ocean? Create something soothing to hear. Then listen for a few moments using your imaginary sense of hearing. (Pause here.)

Next use your imaginary sense of smell. Notice whatever scents you can detect, or choose to smell something soothing from your scene. Take a few moments to use your imaginary sense of smell. (Pause here.)

Next notice if you can feel anything with your imaginary sense of touch. What are you sitting on or where are you standing in your scene? Can you feel anything? Choose to feel something soothing in your scene. Take a few moments to use your imaginary sense of touch. (Pause here.)

Finally, use your imaginary sense of taste. Are you eating or drinking anything in this scene? Choose something soothing to taste. Then take a few moments to use your imaginary sense of taste. (Pause here.)

Now take a few more moments to explore your safe place using all of your imaginary senses. Recognize how safe and relaxed you feel here. Remember, you can come back to this place in your imagination whenever you need to feel safe and relaxed. You can also come back whenever you're feeling distressed or you need to prepare yourself to do something difficult. Look around one last time to remember what your scene looks like. Now keep your eyes closed and return your focus to your breathing. Then, when you feel ready, open your eyes and return your focus to the room.

YOUR EMOTIONS

Learning how to relax and deal with stress also requires that you learn to effectively cope with your emotions. Emotions are signals in your body that tell you something is happening. When something pleasant is happening, you feel happy, and when something unpleasant is happening, you feel distressed. Unfortunately, many people find it difficult or impossible to recognize their emotional experiences, even if they are pleasant ones. This can happen for many reasons.

For example, when some people were children, they were severely scolded or invalidated whenever they had emotional experiences, and as a result, they learned how to turn off their emotions. (Maybe they were frequently told to "shut up," "stop crying," or "grow up.") Then, as adolescents or adults, they continued to ignore their emotions or repress them out of habit. Similarly, other people avoid their emotions because they've been the victim of some type of trauma, such as a bad relationship, an accident, or some kind of abuse. So now they find ways to distance themselves from their painful emotional experiences by being critical of themselves and others, obsessing over minute details, avoiding activities, or using alcohol or drugs to numb themselves.

From time to time we all put our emotions on temporary hold without causing ourselves much difficulty. However, cutting yourself off from your emotions on a regular basis can cause big problems in your life. Imagine if your emotional experiences were like basketballs, and each time you felt an emotion, you just stuffed it into a closet. Eventually, there wouldn't be any room left in the closet, and either your emotions would come bursting out or you'd have to find something else to do with them, like build another closet. But no matter what you did, you'd probably feel more anxious and stressed-out than when the original emotional event took place.

Something similar happens to many people who struggle with personality disorders. For example, Olivia has obsessive-compulsive personality disorder, and whenever she has an unpleasant emotional experience, like an argument with her husband, she distances herself from the incident by roaming the neighborhood and collecting useless objects she finds on the street. So now, in addition to the distress she experiences with her husband, she has the further problem of a very cluttered home. Similarly, Vivian, who has personality disorder not otherwise specified, often feels unappreciated by her boss. So after work, she frequently goes to a bar and drinks in order to numb her feelings. Now, in addition to having difficulties at work, she has a problem with alcohol.

If you're like Olivia or Vivian, you might not notice many of your emotions because you have them turned off most of the time. However, in order to learn how your emotions are influencing your thoughts and behaviors—and the habits of your personality disorder—you need to learn how to turn them back on and experience them. Remember, just because you don't notice your emotions, that doesn't mean they've disappeared; it just means that your emotions have control over you that you're not even aware of.

Develop Emotional Awareness Skills

As you might have guessed, emotional awareness is the ability to notice and accurately judge how you're feeling. For many people with personality disorders this can be difficult. That's why these skills are so important to learn. Emotional awareness skills serve four purposes. They can help you to:

1. Identify your emotions

2. Describe your emotions

3. Be mindful of your emotions without judging them

4. Engage in pleasant emotional activities, especially when you're feeling overwhelmed

Let's look at an example. Hillary, who has histrionic personality disorder, was at lunch with a group of friends when she noticed that no one was talking to her or paying attention to her. Suddenly, without thinking about it, Hillary turned to a stranger sitting at the next table and began flirting with him. Her actions made both the stranger and her friends feel very uncomfortable. In this situation, Hillary wasn't aware that she was feeling lonely and scared or that she was behaving seductively to get attention.

Remember, your thoughts, feelings, and behaviors all influence each other. If Hillary had known how to use emotional awareness skills, she could have identified what she was feeling, and then, if she needed to distract herself from how uncomfortable she was feeling, she could have engaged in some type of pleasant emotional experience, like stepping outside the restaurant for a breath of fresh air.

Emotional awareness skills are also important to learn because in chapter 11 you'll build on these skills when you learn how to use emotion exposure, which is a tool that will help you learn how to confront your distressing emotions.

Identify Your Emotional Experiences

The first step in building emotional awareness is to recognize when you're feeling an emotion. This might be difficult if you've developed the habit of suppressing your emotions or distracting yourself from them. There are many ways to do this and here are two exercises to begin. If you feel too anxious to do one of these exercises, try using a stress-reduction technique before, while, or after you do the exercise. (For example, you might do five minutes of mindful breathing before you watch a movie that you know will arouse an emotional response.) Also, if you start to feel overwhelmed by your emotions while doing any of these exercises, stop and relax. Use a technique that helps you reconnect with your physical body, such as progressive muscle relaxation, especially if you start to feel disconnected from reality, your thoughts, or your body—a condition that is called *dissociation*.

EXERCISE: Keep an Emotional Journal

To begin identifying your emotions, try keeping an Emotional Journal. Make photocopies of the following blank form and keep a copy with you throughout your day. Then start recording any feelings that you notice. Or if that's too difficult, practice by picking a situation that happened to you recently and record how you felt when it occurred. If you don't know exactly how you felt or you don't know the words to describe it, try describing it as a sound (such as arrgh or ugh), a color (like deep red or emerald green), a physical feeling (such as tightness in the neck), or any other way that makes sense to you. Whatever you do is okay, as long as it helps you to identify that something significant happened that caused you to feel something.

The more you practice identifying and describing your emotions, the easier the process will become. If you're still not sure how you felt but you know you probably felt something, just record the event and come back to it later. Maybe your emotion will become clearer to you later in the day. When writing in your Emotional Journal, do your best to identify your feelings, thoughts, and actions. Record the following:

- What happened

- How you felt

- What you thought or said

- What you did

Record something in your Emotional Journal every day for at least two weeks or until you start noticing your emotions more regularly.

Here's an Emotional Journal example filled out by Scott, who struggles with schizotypal personality disorder.

EMOTIONAL JOURNAL—Scott's Example

What happened?	How did you feel? (Do your best to describe it.)	What did you think or say?	What did you do?
Wed., my colleagues asked me to dinner after work.	I had a tight feeling in my stomach, like I wanted to vomit.	I wanted to run out of the office after work. I said I'd think about it, but I knew that I wouldn't go.	I made up an excuse to get out of it, which made me feel bad because I was lying to them.
Thurs., someone yelled at me on the street because of the pants I was wearing.	I felt embarrassed.	I thought about running into a store so no one could see me.	I went into the store and waited for people on the street to go away.
Fri., I laughed at a joke that someone made at a party, but no one else thought it was funny.	Ugh. I don't know how to describe it. It was just a bad feeling.	What's wrong with me sometimes?	I left the party early to go home.
Sat., I thought I saw something out of the corner of my eye, but when I turned to look it wasn't there.	I don't know how I felt, but it was strange. If my feeling was a color, it would be yellow and purple.	Am I seeing things, or was it really there?	I ignored it and went on with my day.
Sun., I was in line at the grocery store.	I felt out of place with all those people.	Why do I always feel so out of place?	I paid for my groceries and went home to be alone.

EMOTIONAL JOURNAL

What happened?	How did you feel? (Do your best to describe it.)	What did you think or say?	What did you do?

EXERCISE: Practice Having Emotional Responses

Another way to learn to identify your emotions is to practice having them. In the privacy of your own home or anywhere else that you feel safe, try one of the following activities and allow yourself to experience the emotion that results:

- Watch a powerful movie or television show, whether it's sad, heroic, beautiful, tragic, or touching in some other way.

- Listen to music that triggers an emotional reaction in you.

- Read a poem aloud that you find interesting.

- Look at artwork that stirs a response in you.

- Imagine being in a location that holds some importance for you (like your favorite beach, city, or memorial, the place where you were born, and so forth).

- Imagine meeting someone who is special to you or whom you greatly admire.

- Imagine having a special event take place in your life (like a party in your honor, your favorite team winning the championship, getting married, and so forth).

While doing this exercise, do your best to pay attention to whatever stirs inside you. As you did in the last exercise, do your best to describe your emotional experience using words, sounds, colors, or other descriptive terms. Again, the more you practice this, the easier it will become.

EXERCISE: Describe Your Emotions

After you've had some success identifying your emotional experiences, you can further enhance your understanding of them by taking the time to describe an emotion in as much detail as possible. To begin, pick an emotion. It can be either a pleasant or an unpleasant one. Ideally, you should choose one that you're feeling right now, unless that emotion is overwhelmingly sad or self-destructive. If it is, you should wait until you feel more in control of your emotions before beginning this exercise. On the other hand, if you can't identify what you're feeling now, choose an emotion that you were feeling recently, something that you can easily remember.

To help you choose an emotion, or to describe it more accurately, use the following list of some commonly felt emotions.

List of Commonly Felt Emotions

Afraid	Guilty	Sad
Angry	Happy	Scared
Annoyed	Hopeful	Secure
Anxious	Hopeless	Shy
Bored	Hurt	Smart
Cheerful	Irritated	Sorry
Confident	Jealous	Strong
Curious	Joyful	Surprised
Depressed	Lively	Suspicious
Disappointed	Lonely	Terrified
Embarrassed	Loved	Thrilled
Energetic	Mad	Tired
Enthusiastic	Nervous	Unsure
Excited	Obsessed	Vulnerable
Flirtatious	Proud	Worried
Foolish	Regretful	Worthless
Frustrated	Relieved	Worthy

When you have identified the emotion you want to explore, write it down at the top of a piece of paper. Then use your imagination to be as creative as possible in your exploration of the emotion. For example:

- Draw a picture of what your emotion might look like.

- Think of a sound that would further describe it.

- Describe an action that is related to it.

- Describe the intensity of the emotion.

- Describe the overall quality of what it feels like.

- Add anything else that comes to mind.

Be Mindful of Your Emotions Without Judgment

You've already learned how to breathe mindfully, observe your judgments, and identify your emotions. Now it's time to combine those skills and learn to be mindful of your emotions without judging your experience. This exercise is important because it can prevent your distressing emotions from becoming overwhelming and painful.

During this exercise, focus on whatever emotion you are feeling at the time. Or if you can't identify feeling one, recall a recent event in which you did have an emotional experience and do your best to visualize as many details of that scene as possible. Then, while you're focusing on your emotion, notice any judgments that arise. As you notice them, use one of the following visualizations—or something similar—to imagine your judgments floating away from you:

- Place each judgment on a leaf and watch it float down a stream.

- See each judgment written on a billboard as you pass by in a car.

- See each judgment written on a boxcar in a long train that passes by.

- Place each judgment on a cloud and let it float away.

- Place each judgment in a bottle and watch the ocean sweep the bottles away.

Letting go of judgments can feel strange and difficult at first, but it's very important to learn how to observe your judgments rather than be controlled by them.

EXERCISE: Being Mindful of Your Emotions Without Judging

Read through the script below before you begin doing the exercise and, again, record them if you'd like to listen to them.

Begin with a few minutes of mindful breathing. Notice your breath moving in and out of your body, helping you to feel more relaxed with each breath. While continuing to breathe in a slow, even rhythm, notice the emotion that you're experiencing (or remember an emotion that you recently experienced). Notice where you feel the emotion in your body. Is it in a particular place? Do you experience it as muscle tension somewhere? Notice any other physical sensations connected to your emotion. (Pause here.)

Now become aware of the emotion's strength. Is it strong or weak? Is it growing or diminishing? Is it pleasant or distressing? Try to name the emotion and describe some of its qualities. (Pause here.)

Now notice any thoughts or judgments that arise as a result of your emotion. Especially notice any judgments about yourself or others. Do your best to continue observing your emotion and any thoughts or judgments that arise. (Pause here.)

Now use one of the techniques described above to watch your thoughts and judgments float away. For example, watch each judgment float past on a cloud and let it go. As you do this, you'll probably notice another thought or judgment arising to take its place. That's perfectly normal. Simply allow that thought or judgment to float away as well. (Pause here.)

Continue to observe your emotion and any judgments that arise. Notice how your emotion changes in form and intensity. Notice how frequently thoughts and judgments arise. Just continue to let them float away. (Pause here.)

Recognize that whatever emotion you're feeling is real and legitimate, but also notice that it does not stay the same or have complete control over you. Emotions come and go like waves hitting the shore, and like the ocean's waves, they also rise and fall in intensity. It's normal for emotions to feel powerful sometimes, but that doesn't mean that they stay that way. Often, emotions diminish in strength if we let go of the judgments that surround them.

Continue breathing, observing your emotions, and allowing your thoughts and judgments to float away.

Finish the exercise with a few minutes of mindful breathing, and when you're finished, return your focus to the room.

DISTRACT YOURSELF WITH PLEASURABLE ACTIVITIES

Sometimes engaging in a pleasurable activity is the best way to soothe your distressing emotions and reduce your physical stress. Surprisingly, many people—not only those with personality disorders—have forgotten how to do anything just for fun. If you're one of those people, it's very important that you regularly incorporate some type of pleasure into your life to create a sense of emotional balance.

Pleasurable activities also serve another purpose. Many people with personality disorders frequently feel overwhelmed by distressing emotions such as anger, frustration, and loneliness. When this happens, it's often helpful to temporarily distract yourself from the painful emotion until you're ready to cope with the problem. To borrow a phrase from *The Dialectical Behavior Therapy Skills Workbook,*[63] your plan should be "Distract, relax, and cope." In other words, once you've noticed that you're feeling overwhelmed by a painful emotion, do your best to engage in something pleasurable to distract yourself until you've calmed down enough to deal with the problem successfully. Notice that the plan isn't to avoid your problems completely. This difference is very important.

Go back to chapter 4 and take another look at the Big List of Pleasurable Activities. Find some activities you'd be willing to try, and then take time out of each day to engage in at least one. In addition, find some activities that you can distract yourself with whenever you feel overwhelmed. Mark those you can do at home (H) and those you can do if you're away from home (A). Then keep a list of these pleasurable activities with you so that you can easily refer to it wherever you are.

STAY HEALTHY

Your physical health will also influence your ability to relax and reduce stress in your life. For example, without the proper nutrients from your diet, your body might not be able to support a healthy lifestyle. For dietary recommendations, consult your medical professional or check out the U.S. Department of Agriculture's "My Pyramid" website, www.mypyramid.gov. There you'll find healthy meal plans, tips for eating out, and lots of information about eating right.

A healthy body and a well-balanced state of mind also depend on regular physical exercise. Some studies have even shown exercise to be an effective treatment for depression.[65] Choose an activity that you enjoy, so you'll stick with it. But before beginning any exercise routine, be sure to consult your medical professional for a physical exam and exercise guidelines.

REMIND YOURSELF TO RELAX

Now that you've worked through all the stress-reduction and relaxation techniques, note the ones that worked best for you and record them below. Then write them on a small piece of paper that you can keep with you (for example, in your wallet, handbag, or backpack) so that you can remember what to do when you're feeling anxious, worried, or stressed.

1. _____

2. _____

3. _____

4. _____

5. _____

IN CONCLUSION

Mental strain and physical tension affect everyone. But for those who are already struggling with the effects of a personality disorder, the additional effects of stress can be overwhelming. That's why it's important to practice stress-reduction and relaxation techniques every day, so you can use them whenever you need to relax, focus, or do something challenging. Find the techniques that work best for you and keep a list of those techniques with you to use whenever you're feeling stressed or overwhelmed.

CHAPTER 8

Develop Problem-Solving Skills

In order to effectively improve the habits associated with your personality disorder, it's necessary to learn a variety of specific coping skills. There are many skills that you could learn depending on the types of issues you're struggling with. This chapter will teach you an effective coping skill to solve difficult problems.

Have you ever been stuck in a difficult situation and you just didn't know what to do? Did you freeze? Did you feel anxious or scared? Did your mind go blank? Did you procrastinate, or did you just completely avoid dealing with the situation? These are common responses of those who lack problem-solving skills. Learning some problem-solving skills will help you to identify and select healthy, effective solutions to difficult, anxiety-provoking situations.

The technique outlined here is based on the work of Thomas D'Zurilla and Marv Goldfried[66] as well as the book *Thoughts & Feelings.*[57]

THE FIVE STEPS OF PROBLEM SOLVING

The five steps of problem solving can be easily remembered by using the acronym SOLVE. These are the steps:

1. **S**tate your problem.

2. **O**utline your solutions.

3. **L**ist your strategies.

4. **V**iew the consequences of your strategies.

5. **E**valuate the results.

At first sight, this technique may look like a very lengthy process just to solve a single problem, but it will get easier and faster with practice. And more importantly, your problems will become less frightening to confront and you'll be able to cope with them more effectively. Eventually, with enough practice, you'll memorize the process and be able to mentally go through it in just a few seconds. Remember, part of the problem associated with personality disorders is that you often use the same limited set of strategies, whether or not they are successful. Take this opportunity to learn a new technique that will help you to think more creatively.

Step 1: State Your Problem

The first step to solving any problem is to identify what the problem is and when it occurs. This might be easy for you. Perhaps you experience the same problem on a regular basis, such as "Every day, when I ask my coworker for help, she ignores me." Or maybe the problem happens less frequently, such as "Whenever I visit my parents, they always ask me annoying questions, like when am I going to get married." Even if you don't have an immediate problem that needs solving, this skill is important to learn. Consider practicing this technique on a problem that has already passed or already been solved.

Below, you'll find a list of common difficulties for which people often need problem-solving skills. Use this list to think of some problems you might be willing to work with to solve, and remember, in the beginning it's often helpful to practice this technique on an easier problem that has fewer distressing consequences, before trying to cope with a more difficult issue:

- Health issues (such as illness, weight, sleep, diet, exercise, and mental health)

- Finances (such as bills, debt, and expenses)

- Work (such as an unsatisfying job, no job, poor pay, a bad boss, and difficult coworkers)

- Living arrangements (such as a bad neighborhood, bad neighbors, and too small a home)

- Relationships (such as lonely, unsatisfying relationships and lack of romance)

- Recreation (such as not enough time, lack of ideas, and equipment that's too expensive)

- Family (such as conflicts, insecurity, lack of intimacy, and children's issues)

- Other (such as bad habits, lack of motivation, lack of goals, and lack of spirituality)

Now, using this list or your own ideas, pick three problems you'd like to solve that are respectivly easier, more moderate, and harder in terms of the difficulties they present. Begin practicing this skill with the easier issue and, as you gain confidence in your ability to solve problems, then try to solve the moderate and harder problems.

What three problems have you identified?

- Easier: _____

- Moderate: _____

- Difficult: _____

Starting with your easier problem, fill out the Problem Analysis Worksheet to gain a better understanding of how it's affecting you. Use Scarlett's example worksheet if you need help.

Problem Analysis Worksheet

What is the problem? _____

_____

Who is involved? _____

_____

What happens? What bothers you? _____

_____

Where does the problem occur? _____

_____

When does it occur? _____

_____

How does it happen? (Is there a pattern?) _____

_____

Why do you think it happens? _____

_____

What else is important in this situation? _____

_____

_____

How do you respond to the situation? (List your behaviors.) _____

_____

How does it make you feel? _____

_____

What outcome do you want to see in this situation? _____

_____

_____

Reprinted with permission by New Harbinger Publications, Inc. From *Thoughts and Feelings*, by McKay, Davis, and Fanning (1997).

Problem Analysis Worksheet—Scarlett's Example

What is the problem?

Every time I go to family gatherings, my parents nag me with questions about my life and my relationships, and I don't know what to tell them.

Who is involved?

Me, my father, and my mother.

What happens? What bothers you?

They ask me lots of questions, and they won't listen when I tell them that I don't want to talk about it.

Where does the problem occur?

Anyplace where I meet my family, mainly at my parents' house.

When does it occur?

Anytime I meet them.

How does it happen? (Is there a pattern?)

One of my parents will ask how I've been and how is work, and then they proceed to ask about my friends and why I'm not dating anyone.

Why do you think it happens?

Sometimes I think they're just being nosy, and other times I think they only care about me and want me to be happy.

What else is important in this situation?

My mother's health is not good, and I don't want to make it worse.

How do you respond to the situation? (List your behaviors.)

I leave the room, I argue with them, or I just shut up and don't say anything.

How does it make you feel?

Angry, confused, and hurt.

What outcome do you want to see in this situation?

I care about my parents and want to continue seeing them, but I just wish they would leave me alone and stop bothering me about my life and my lack of relationships.

Step 2: Outline Your Solutions

Now that you've identified your problem and completed the related worksheet, it's time to identify the best possible solutions to your problem. Be creative when thinking of solutions. Some of them might not seem achievable right now, but leave yourself open to using the best strategies possible. Often your solutions are related to your last three responses on the worksheet—what you do, how you feel, and what you want.

In Scarlett's example, she realized that she cared about her parents, especially her ill mother, and she wanted to enjoy her visits with them instead of feeling upset. Based on her last three responses on her Problem Analysis Worksheet, she set forth the following three possible solutions:

A. *Figure out better ways to deal with my parents' questions about my life.*

B. *Learn how to relax when I'm around them.*

C. *Set rules with my parents for my visits.*

When setting your goals, keep two things in mind. First, describe what you do want to happen, rather than what you don't want to happen. For example, rather than saying, "I don't want to get angry," rephrase your goal as, "I do want to feel calmer." This will make your goal more positive, specific, and easier to achieve. Second, state your goal from your own point of view. For example, rather than saying, "I don't want my parents to get angry with me all the time," restate it as, "I want to figure out how to develop a better relationship with my parents." The difference is important because it gives you more control of your goal, rather than relying on someone else's thoughts and actions.

Based on your own Problem Analysis Worksheet, what are three possible solutions to your problem?

A. _____

B. _____

C. _____

Step 3: List Your Strategies

You've probably heard the term "brainstorming," but did you know this technique was created by advertising manager Alex Osborn to help generate new, creative ideas for advertisements?[67] Now you can use the same creative technique to think of strategies that will help you to achieve the solutions you recorded in step 2. But in order to brainstorm effectively, it's important to follow four basic rules:

1. **Don't criticize your ideas.** Record as many strategies as you can think of without judging them as being either good or bad.

2. **Generate lots of ideas.** The more possible strategies you can think of, the greater your chances are of finding the solution that works. If you can, make a long list of ideas.

3. **Generate creative, even silly, ideas.** Don't censor yourself. Think as creatively as possible. The crazier or sillier the idea is, the better. Have fun with your thinking. You might come up with something original and effective that you never thought of before.

4. **Combine and improve your ideas, if necessary.** If you create two or more strategies that fit well together, combine them into one great idea.

And remember, while you're brainstorming for overall strategies, you don't need to focus on specific, step-by-step procedures. You can figure that out later. Right now, do your best to think of general strategies for each of your solutions. For example, here are Scarlett's brainstorming lists:

SCARLETT'S POSSIBLE SOLUTION A: "FIGURE OUT BETTER WAYS TO DEAL WITH MY PARENTS' QUESTIONS ABOUT MY LIFE."

1.   Hire television's Dr. Phil for family therapy.

2.   Read a book on family relationships.

3.   Read a book on hostage negotiating.

4.   Tell them, "My life is none of your business."

5.   Write them a letter to them explaining how I feel about their questions.

6.   Draw a picture showing them how their questions make me feel.

7.   Take a meditation class to help me calm down.

8.   Hire an actor to visit them with me as my "boyfriend."

9.   Get a dog to keep me company and bring it with me when I visit.

10. Ask a coworker how she deals with her family's questions.

SCARLETT'S POSSIBLE SOLUTION B: "LEARN HOW TO RELAX WHEN I'M AROUND THEM."

1.   Take a meditation class.

2.   Take a yoga class.

3.   Swim more often.

4.   Breathe deeply.

5.   Take a tranquilizer before I visit.

6.   Imagine them sitting in their underwear while they're nagging me.

7.   Meditate, pray, and swim before each visit.

8.   Ask them to sit outside with me while I visit, so I can relax.

9.   Learn how to communicate with them more effectively (book? class?).

10. Smile and tell them I'm happy living alone.

SCARLETT'S POSSIBLE SOLUTION C: "SET RULES WITH
MY PARENTS FOR MY VISITS."

1. *Tell them I won't visit as often if they keep nagging me.*

2. *Explain how I feel over a meal at a nice restaurant.*

3. *Tell them I'll let them know when I have a boyfriend.*

4. *Tell them they can ask me personal questions only once a month.*

5. *Tell them all requests for information must be made in writing.*

6. *Ask Dr. Phil to mediate the situation.*

7. *Make all of us see a family therapist for a few visits.*

8. *Have all of us read the same book on effective communication skills.*

9. *Ask Aunt Mary to explain to them how I feel about their questions.*

10. *Send them an e-mail explaining what I want.*

EXERCISE: Brainstorm Strategies for Your Three Possible Solutions

Now do the same thing for each of the three solutions that you thought of earlier: A, B, and C. Brainstorm at least ten possible strategies for each one. Make sure you record your ideas in the space below, rather than just trying to remember them. And don't give up. Take your time. Creating a list might take you ten minutes, an hour, or even a day or two, but however long it takes is fine.

The Brainstorm List of Possible Strategies

What is the problem? _____

Possible solution A: _____

1. _____

2. _____

3. _____

4. _____

5. _____

6. _____

7. _____

8. _____

9. _____

10. _____

Possible solution B: _____

1. _____

2. _____

3. _____

4. _____

5. _____

6. _____

7. _____

8. _____

9. _____

10. _____

Possible solution C: _____

1. _____

2. _____

3. _____

4. _____

5. _____

6. _____

7. _____

8. _____

9. _____

10. _____

Step 4: View the Consequences of Your Strategies

At this point in the problem-solving process, you should have recorded your problem, three solutions (A, B, and C), and ten possible strategies for achieving each solution (thirty strategies in total). Now it's time to narrow down your list of strategies and to evaluate the possible consequences of using them.

From your three lists of strategies for solutions A, B, and C, choose the best solution. Base your decision on common sense. For example, perhaps solution A has the best strategies, but solution C has the most realistic strategies. Look at the three lists and pick the solution that strikes you as having the best chance of succeeding.

Next, using the solution you picked (A, B, or C), narrow down the number of strategies from ten to three. Pick your three best strategies for that solution. Combine multiple good ideas into one great idea. Cross out unrealistic or outlandish ideas (like getting Dr. Phil to help).

Then, to evaluate the consequences of each strategy, divide a blank piece of paper in half. At the top of the paper, record the first strategy that you are evaluating. On the left side of the paper, write down the possible positive consequences of using that strategy, and on the right side, record the possible negative consequences. Do this for all three strategies.

While evaluating the consequences, consider how each strategy will positively and negatively affect:

- You

- Others

- Your long-term goals

- Your short-term goals

Hopefully, after you've evaluated the positive and negative consequences of each of the three strategies, one of them will clearly emerge as the best way to resolve your problem. This will then become the strategy that you'll put into action to solve your problem. However, if this doesn't happen, you might consider grading each of the consequences on a scale of 1 to 4. Then you can add up the scores on both the positive and negative sides to see how the outcome might affect you.

Let's look at Scarlett's evaluations. She thought solution A was the most effective for her problem: "Figure out better ways to deal with my parents' questions about my life." She chose the following three strategies to evaluate and graded them (in parentheses).

Scarlett's Evaluation Example

Strategy 1: Write them a letter explaining how I feel about their questions.

Positive Consequences	**Negative Consequences**
My thoughts will be clearer. (4)	*I might hurt their feelings. (3)*
I can take my time. (4)	*They might not understand. (2)*
It might improve our relationship in the long run. (3)	
Score:　　11	5

Strategy 2: Take a meditation class to help me calm down.

Positive Consequences	**Negative Consequences**
It will help me relax in general. (4)	*It won't help them relax. (3)*
I'll be able to communicate with them better. (3)	*They don't know what meditation is. (3)*
Score:　　7	6

Strategy 3: Read a book on family relationships.

Positive Consequences	**Negative Consequences**
I might learn new skills. (3)	*It won't help if they don't read it, too. (4)*
I might learn what's wrong. (2)	*I might still be frustrated. (4)*
Maybe they would read the book. (1)	
Score:　　6	8

After evaluating the strategies and looking at the scores, Scarlett realized that strategy 1 was the best solution because its positive consequences (a score of 11) clearly outweighed its negative consequences (a score of only 5).

Step 5: Evaluate Your Results

Once you've chosen a strategy, you'll need to put it into action. In Scarlett's example, the action was to write her parents a letter, but she needed to break it down into easier steps, such as:

1. *Set aside time to write the letter.*

2. *Hold on to the letter for one week to make revisions.*

3. *Give the letter to my parents to read.*

4. Meet with them to hear their reaction and discuss it.

If you are have trouble putting your own solution into action, try brainstorming again to figure out the steps you'll need to take. If you feel nervous or scared about trying this procedure, use one of the stress-reduction techniques to help you relax before doing it. Or if you feel intimidated about talking to someone, wait until you learn assertive communications skills in chapter 9.

Then, after you've taken action, evaluate the results. Did the chosen strategy help you to solve the problem? Did you at least move closer to solving the problem? If not, what went wrong? Try the same strategy again if necessary. Or pick a different strategy to put into action. Go back over your list of solutions A, B, and C. Do you now see a more effective strategy? If your answer is yes, try that one. If it is no, go back to step 3 and brainstorm new, creative ways to solve your problem. Don't be ashamed or afraid to keep trying. Remember, you're breaking yourself from old habits and learning new ones, and sometimes that takes a great deal of time and practice.

IN CONCLUSION

Problem solving is hard for everyone, not just people who are struggling with personality disorders. Take your time to learn this skill, and it will become a powerful tool you can use for the rest of your life.

CHAPTER 9

Develop Assertive Communication Skills

For many people with personality disorders, one of their core problems is the lack of effective communication skills. For example, you might have trouble (1) asking others for help, (2) saying no to people who ask you to do things you don't want to do, or (3) asking to have your needs met in an appropriate way. However, as difficult as these problems are for you, the good news is that effective communication skills are easy to learn; they just take practice.

The most important communication skill to learn is assertiveness. Assertiveness training will help you to:

- Learn to communicate more effectively

- Express your thoughts and feelings more easily

- Get your needs met in appropriate ways without violating the rights of others

- Stop being passive or aggressive

- Deal with criticism in a helpful way

- Learn how to set appropriate boundaries with others

Assertiveness is not a trait with which most people are born; it's a skill that we all need to learn, and no one is assertive all the time. One of the blocks to being assertive is that some people don't think that they have the right to ask for the things they need, to sometimes put themselves first, to occasionally inconvenience others, or to express their opinions. However, the truth is that you do have a right to all of these things, and hopefully assertive communication skills will help you to realize that.

The exercises in this chapter will require a few weeks of practice. Most of the exercises described here come from *Messages: The Communication Skills Book*, by Matthew McKay, Martha Davis, and Patrick Fanning, and you should consult this book for other specific communication skills, such as effective listening skills, nonverbal skills, job interviewing skills, and public speaking skills.[68]

PASSIVE COMMUNICATION STYLE

In contrast to being assertive, some people use either a passive or an aggressive style of communication. Here's an example of being passive: Britney, who struggled with borderline personality disorder, often felt alone and frequently worried that her friends would abandon her. As a result, she often behaved in a passive way with her friends because she was afraid that if she did anything to upset them, they would desert her.

One day Britney was planning to stay home and do some schoolwork, but her friend Adam called and asked her to give him a ride to the shopping mall. Britney was afraid to tell him no, so she put aside her own work to drive him. She resented Adam for asking for a ride, but she didn't want to say no to his request. Because she didn't want to anger him or risk losing his friendship, it seemed easier for her to put aside her own needs. But over the next few days, Adam continued asking Britney for favors and her frustration and anger levels grew. Then, suddenly, one day she couldn't take it anymore. Seemingly out of the blue Britney lashed out at Adam when he requested another favor, telling him to leave her alone. Adam was stunned because he hadn't known that anything was wrong. Britney's anger was a complete surprise to him, and for the next three weeks he didn't call her.

In this example, Britney behaved so passively because she was trying to maintain her relationship with Adam at the expense of her own needs. However, by responding passively rather than saying no, her actions actually put their relationship in jeopardy because she eventually became so frustrated and angry with Adam that he stopped speaking to her.

People who use a passive style similar to Britney's often behave in the following ways:

- They don't speak up for their own needs or ask for what they want.

- They don't express their feelings.

- They have trouble saying no to others' requests.

- They are shy about speaking or they speak in a very soft voice that is hard to hear.

- They try to communicate indirectly, such as by frowning or sighing.

- They run away from their relationships after becoming frustrated.

AGGRESSIVE COMMUNICATION STYLE

Here's an example of using an aggressive style of communication: Anthony, who struggled with antisocial personality disorder, thought he was smarter and more deserving than most people, so he didn't care if other people suffered because of his actions. One day at the office, his coworker Dave asked for help carrying some heavy books. Anthony immediately became angered by Dave's request. Anthony had already set aside this time for lunch and he didn't want to be bothered. "People are always pissing me off," he thought to himself. However, instead of explaining to Dave that he had already made plans, Anthony became aggressive.

First, he called Dave an idiot for always bothering him and not being able to do the job himself. Then he told Dave that he wasn't going to help. While Dave was walking away from Anthony's desk, he tripped and fell. Anthony laughed and immediately attacked Dave with insults: "You're such a klutz, Dave. You should go back to your old job of mopping floors." Dave walked away feeling very hurt and upset.

In this example, Anthony behaved very aggressively. In contrast to Britney, he was able to speak up for his own needs, but he did so in a completely inappropriate way, which attacked and insulted Dave. Obviously, this style of communication is not effective for creating healthy relationships either.

People who use an aggressive style similar to Anthony's often behave in the following ways:

- They frequently think they're right and others are wrong.

- They have strong opinions about the way others "should" behave.

- They become aggressive when another person's request is seen as an inconvenience.

- They seek to punish others.

- They try to control the behavior of others.

- They insult others and are frequently sarcastic.

EXERCISE: Identify Your Own Style of Communication

To help you identify the style of communication that you rely on, try the following exercise taken from *The Dialectical Behavior Therapy Skills Workbook*.[63] Think back over recent interactions in some of your significant relationships, and then place a check mark next to the statements that reflect your typical behavior:

1. I go along with something, even if I don't like it.

2. I push people to do what's right, even if it bothers them.

3. I try to be pleasant and easygoing, no matter what people do or say.

4. I'm not afraid to get angry with people when they deserve it.

5. I always try to be sensitive to what other people need and feel, even if my own needs get lost in the process.

6. I know what I want and insist on getting it.

7. When there's a conflict, I tend to give in and let things go the other person's way.

8. When people don't do what's right, I don't let them get away with it.

9. I'll pull away from a relationship rather than say anything that could be upsetting.

10. You can't let people continue being selfish or stupid; you have to set them straight so they'll see what they're doing.

11. I prefer to just leave people alone.

12. If people ignore my needs or insist on things that don't work for me, I get more and more upset until they pay attention to what I want.

Which numbers did you check? If you tended to check the odd numbers, your predominant style is passive; if you checked the even numbers, you have an aggressive communication style.

Now based on the style of communication that you use, answer the following questions. Be as honest as you can.

• What are the advantages of using your style of communication (either passive or aggressive)?

_____

_____

• What are the disadvantages?

_____

_____

• What would be the advantages of being able to ask for what you want in a new, more effective way?

_____

_____

BEING ASSERTIVE

In between being passive and aggressive there is a middle way of communicating; it's called being assertive. Here's an example of being assertive: Nathan struggled with narcissistic personality disorder, but he'd been practicing his assertive communication skills. One day he needed help from his coworker Beth. In the past, he would have just given her an order and expected her to follow it. But he'd recently learned that this type of aggressive communication put a lot of strain on their relationship, so he used his assertiveness skills instead. Here's what happened.

Nathan had been asked to organize a luncheon for a new client, but he felt nervous because he'd never done this before. However, Beth had successfully organized several luncheons, and Nathan wanted her help. Nathan went to her desk and said, "Hi Beth. As you might know, I've been asked to organize this luncheon, but I feel nervous about it. I was hoping you'd be able to help me." Beth replied she wasn't sure if she would have the time, and she was too busy at the moment to discuss it further. In response, Nathan said, "I understand you're busy right now, but I would really appreciate your help. Can we discuss this later in the day when you have more time?" Beth said yes, and later that day she agreed to help organize the event.

In this example, Nathan effectively described the facts of the situation, how he felt about it, and what he wanted. He also listened very well to Beth and heard her concerns. His doing that put Beth at ease and allowed her to respond to his request in an honest way.

People who use an assertive style of communication often behave in the following ways:

- They make direct statements about their thoughts, feelings, and needs.

- They get their needs met by stating them in a kind but firm way.

- They are considerate of other people's needs and their feelings.

- They can say no to others when it's necessary.

- They listen attentively to others.

- They can negotiate conflicts in an effective manner without being aggressive or simply giving in.

People who are assertive also appear to be very confident because of their body language. For example, they maintain good posture and stand a little straighter than others when speaking. Their voices are relaxed, clear, and loud enough to be understood. And their eyes maintain regular contact with the other person, rather than staring at the ground or looking away.

EXERCISE: Your Assertive Goals

If you could act and communicate assertively, what would you like to do? With your answer to that question in mind, pick five goals. Ideally, you'll pick five goals that you can reasonably initiate in the near future. For example, it might be unreasonable to say, "I'd ask my brother for the money he owes me," if you don't expect to speak with your brother for the next six months. It might be more reasonable, and better practice, to keep your goals simple and achievable in the near future, such as "This weekend I'll ask my friend for a favor, like driving me to the supermarket." Setting your goals for the near future will make them easier to set up and practice.

Also, vary the difficulty of the goals you pick. Think of your goals in relation to a difficulty scale of 1 to 10, with 10 being extremely difficult and 1 being very easy. Pick five goals that vary in degree of difficulty, such as 2, 3, 6, 7, and 9.

In addition, be aware of goals that include family members or close friends. These are often more difficult. For nearly everyone, confronting a family member or a close friend about a problem or a past hurt will more than likely be graded a 9 or 10 in difficulty. Be sure to pick easier situations to master before being assertive with family members.

Lastly, construct your goals using "I statements." Remember, the only person you have any control over is yourself. You can't force another person to do anything, so focus on yourself. For example, it would be unreasonable to say, "Jim should grow up and take responsibility for his own life." In reality, you can't force Jim to "grow up" or to do anything else. A more reasonable goal would be, "I'm going to tell Jim how his actions are affecting me and what my responses will be if he doesn't change." This goal highlights actions you have control over. Equally important, this goal is stated in a nonblaming way. Assertive statements should never attack or blame another person. Doing that only causes the other person to become defensive, and this makes it more difficult to achieve your goal. Think of the most nonthreatening, polite way you can express your assertive goal, and you'll be more likely to get what you want.

If you need help thinking of some goals, consider the following ideas:

- The next time someone asks you for something unreasonable, say no. (For example, tell your friend you can't drop everything you're doing to drive him to the shopping mall.)

- Express your opinion or thoughts to someone. (For example, suggest a movie to see with a friend and explain why you want to see it.)

- Ask someone for a simple favor. (For example, ask a friend to bring you a glass of water.)

- Ask someone to stop doing something that bothers you. (For example, ask your husband to slow down while he's driving with you in the car.)

- Ask someone to help you in some way. (For example, ask a neighbor to help you carry some heavy packages.)

- Ask someone to return something of yours. (For example, ask your friend to return the tools that he borrowed and never returned.)

- Ask for something that you deserve or have been waiting for. (For example, ask your boss for your overdue raise.)

- Do something that protects your rights. (For example, return a defective product to a store.)

- Do something that protects your dignity. (For example, tell someone who criticizes you to stop.)

Use the following Assertiveness Goals Chart to list your five goals.

Assertiveness Goals Chart

	Goal (Use a nonblaming "I statement")	Date of Attempt (When will you attempt to achieve this goal? Be as specific as possible.)	Difficulty (Use a 1-10 scale and pick goals that vary in difficulty.)
1			
2			
3			
4			
5			

HOW TO MAKE AN ASSERTIVE STATEMENT

Now that you've identified your assertive goals, let's discuss how you'll get what you want. When you state something in an assertive way, you do so very clearly and directly, without violating the rights of the other person. In comparison, people who communicate in a passive way often beat around the bush, which means they don't say what they want in a clear, direct way. And those who communicate in an aggressive way often insult others. Here are some comparative examples.

	Nonassertive Statement	Assertive Statement
1	"Um, I was wondering if it would be okay if I could, um, return this shirt. If that's okay."	"Hello. This shirt doesn't fit me correctly and it makes me feel uncomfortable. I'd like to return it."
2	"You want me to babysit your kids tonight? Well, I was planning something else, but I guess it's not important. Sure, I'll do it."	"No, I'm sorry. I can't babysit tonight. I already have other plans for this evening, and I would feel awkward if I changed them."
3	"Hi, Melinda. I was wondering, if, like, it would be okay with you, if you could, um, help me with something."	"Hi, Melinda. I was hoping you could help me with the project Mr. Brown assigned in class. I find it very confusing."
4	"Would you shut up? You always come home from work complaining. Stop being so annoying."	"Michael, I'm sorry to interrupt you. But we always talk about the news when you get home, and it always makes me feel depressed. Let's talk about something different at dinner tonight."
5	"So what are you doing this weekend? Nothing? Oh. Okay. I'm not doing anything either. See you later."	"I'm not doing anything this weekend, and if you're free too, I was hoping we could get together. I really enjoy spending time with you."

Notice how much clearer the assertive statements are compared to the nonassertive ones. This is because each assertive statement answers three questions:

1. What's happening in this situation according to your perspective? These are the facts.

2. How does the situation make you feel? These are your feelings.

3. What's the outcome you'd like to see in this situation? These are your needs.

Let's look at the five assertive statements above and see how they fulfill these requirements:

Assertive statement 1

1. Facts: "This shirt doesn't fit me correctly."

2. Feelings: "It makes me feel uncomfortable."

3. Needs: "I'd like to return it."

Assertive statement 2

1. Facts: "I already have other plans for this evening."

2. Feelings: "I would feel awkward if I changed them."

3. Needs: "No, I'm sorry. I can't babysit tonight.

Assertive statement 3

1. Facts: "Mr. Brown assigned a project in class."

2. Feelings: "I find it confusing."

3. Needs: "I was hoping you could help me with the project."

Assertive statement 4

1. Facts: "We always talk about the news when you get home."

2. Feelings: "It makes me feel depressed."

3. Needs: "Let's talk about something different at dinner tonight."

Assertive statement 5

1. Facts: "I'm not doing anything this weekend."

2. Feelings: "I really enjoy spending time with you."

3. Needs: "I was hoping we could get together."

Again, it's important to notice that none of these statements blames the other person in any way and they are not aggressive, even assertive statement number 4. They simply state the speaker's facts and feelings and then make a reasonable request. A good test of any assertive statement is to think about how you would feel if someone else said the same thing to you. Would your statement sound too aggressive? Then use "I statements" and make it less so. Would it be too passive? Then make it more direct and clearer.

EXERCISE: Make Your Own Assertive Statements

Now, for each of the five assertive goals that you identified for yourself, record your own facts, feelings, and needs as best you can.

Goal 1: _____

- Facts: _____

_____

- Feelings: _____
  _____

- Needs: _____
  _____

Goal 2: _____

- Facts: _____
  _____

- Feelings: _____
  _____

- Needs: _____
  _____

Goal 3: _____

- Facts: _____
  _____

- Feelings: _____
  _____

- Needs: _____
  _____

Goal 4: _____

- Facts: _____
  _____

- Feelings: _____
  _____

- Needs: _____
  _____

Goal 5: _____

- Facts: _____
  _____

- Feelings: _____

  _____

- Needs: _____

  _____

Now that you've identified your assertive goals and created your assertive statements, put them aside and continue reading the rest of this chapter. While doing that, identify any of the following strategies that might help you achieve your goals. Then, at the end of this chapter, you'll come back to your list of goals and your assertive statements.

HOW TO LISTEN ASSERTIVELY

Learning how to be assertive includes more than just asking to have your needs met. Each assertive conversation takes place with someone else, and the chances are good that the other person wants something from you, too. This requires you to pay attention and listen to what the other person wants. This is often hard because we human beings do a lot of thinking, and we're often listening to the thoughts in our own heads more than we're listening to the person we're talking to. This can lead to disastrous results when you're trying to be assertive. Despite your best efforts, if you're not really listening to the other person, that person might get so frustrated with you that he or she will just walk away or, even worse, argue with you. Therefore, one very good way of getting what you want from another person is to make sure that person knows you are really listening to what he or she has to say. When you use the following assertive listening skills, the person with whom you're talking will know that he or she has been heard.

Get Ready to Listen

Don't begin a conversation if you're not 100 percent ready to listen to the other person. If you're feeling anxious or thinking too much, try using a stress-reduction technique to calm your body and mind before speaking. Also, ask the other person if he or she is ready to have a conversation with you. Sometimes simply asking, "Is now a good time to talk?" can ensure that both of you are ready. Similarly, if someone asks you to begin a stressful conversation before you're ready, ask if you can discuss it later and set a time. Then stick to your commitment.

Really Listen

Give people the same respect and attention that you'd like them to give to you. Don't just wait for the person to stop talking so that you can say what you're thinking about. Pay attention to what the other person is really saying and feeling. If you're not sure what the other person is saying, feeling, or requesting, then ask the person to be more specific. Say, "I'm not sure that I understand you correctly, can you be more specific?" Or say, "Can you tell me what you want?"

If during a conversation you get lost in your own thoughts or find that your attention is wandering away from what the person is saying, try refocusing on something the person is wearing, like his or her eyeglasses or shirt color. This will help you stay focused on the person you're talking to.

Acknowledge That You're Listening

Throughout the conversation let the other person know that you're really listening to him or her. One good way to do this is to occasionally repeat what you've heard the person say, such as "So what you're saying is that you want me to turn off all the lights before I leave." Also try to acknowledge the other person's feelings, such as "It sounds like this whole situation is making you feel very angry." Acknowledging the other person's thoughts and feelings will also help you to stay focused on the conversation, as well as letting the person know that you really are being attentive.

Take Turns Talking and Listening

No one likes to be in a conversation with someone who does all the talking. So take turns talking and listening. One way to make space and time for the other person to speak is to simply ask, "Is there anything you'd like to say?" Or if you're stuck in a conversation with someone who does all the talking and doesn't let you say anything, ask, "May I interrupt you?"

Listen During Arguments

Taking turns in a conversation is especially important when you're having an argument or a disagreement with someone. During these tough conversations, most people think it's more important to do the talking, but arguments can't be won this way. Instead, let the other person speak and do your best to really listen and acknowledge that you're listening. Then, when it's your turn to speak, make sure you use clear, nonblaming, assertive statements so that the other person will understand your facts, feelings, and needs.

HOW TO HANDLE CRITICISM

Many people have difficulty being assertive for two reasons. The first reason has already been mentioned; namely, that some people think they have no right to ask for what they want. The second reason is that some people are afraid of being criticized if they do ask to have their needs met. This is understandable, but, again, there are solutions to this problem.

There are two ways that people respond to most forms of criticism. Some people become passive when they're criticized because they don't know how to defend themselves or what to say in response. These people often avoid confrontation at all costs. They agree with the people who have criticized them, they become silent, or they escape (or avoid) all situations in which they might be criticized. The result is that they often hold in their anger and resentment, which can lead to depression, thoughts of revenge, or unexpectedly getting angry. Other people respond to criticism with aggressiveness. When someone criticizes them, they lash out at the other person with equal amounts of criticism and insults. The result is that they are frequently angry and are easily irritated. However, there are healthier, more assertive ways to deal with criticism. According to the book *Messages*, three of the best responses are acknowledgment, clouding, and probing.[68]

Acknowledgment

Sometimes good advice sounds like criticism, even when it's helpful and accurate. For example, if your boss or someone you care about points out something that you can improve, such as your work performance or the way you treat others, try to simply acknowledge it rather than getting aggressive or shutting down. For example, compare these two sentences:

- "You're right, Miss Peterson, I do sometimes procrastinate."

- "What do you mean I procrastinate? No I don't. I think I get things done pretty quickly, especially compared to Charles. He takes forever. Why don't you criticize him?"

Obviously, the first sentence sounds more professional and responsible than the second. The person who acknowledges his or her mistakes and shortcomings in a nondefensive way is always seen as more professional and personable than the person who makes excuses. So the next time someone points out something you've done that you can improve—something that you think is accurate in some way—try simply acknowledging it rather than making excuses or apologizing. "Yes, you're right, I could do more chores around the house." "Yes, I was late three times this week." "Yes, I could spend more time with you and the children." Then, after acknowledging these statements, do your best to really improve in those areas.

Clouding

Clouding is a technique you can use to deal with unhelpful criticism that is undeserved, unnecessary, or just plain wrong. *Clouding* means that you partly agree with something that a critic has said to you. Agreeing with the critic in some small way usually satisfies the person and avoids any further argument. This may sound manipulative, but sometimes it's easier to just end the conversation, even if the critic is wrong and you don't agree with what he or she has said.

One way to use clouding is to agree with a small part of the criticism. Listen carefully to what the person is accusing you of and then find some small part that you can agree with, especially a part that might be true. For example:

Critic: How come you always ask me for help? You can never make any decisions by yourself. You're too dependent on other people.

You: Yes, you're right. Sometimes I have trouble making decisions.

Another way to use clouding is to use vague statements like "It could be…" or "You may be right…" These statements leave open the possibility that the critic is right—which satisfies him or her—without you having to really agree with the person. For example:

Critic: You're always too scared to try new things. You need to be braver and take more risks in life.

You: You may be right; maybe I do need to take more risks.

Whatever type of clouding you use, whether it's one of these techniques or one of your own, the principle is the same. Find some way to satisfy your critic to avoid further argument, even if you don't truly agree with what the person has said. And remember, no one is a better authority on you and your behaviors than you are. So just because someone says something bad about you, that doesn't mean it's true.

Probing

Probing requires you to ask questions of the person who's criticizing you in order to find out what's really bothering that person. This might sound intimidating, but the results are often very helpful. Instead of getting stuck in a conflict that confuses you, successful probing can often clarify the situation and lead to some type of solution. You can use this technique when you're not sure whether the person is trying to be helpful or unhelpful or when you don't understand why the person is being critical in the first place.

Try using questions in the form of the next two examples to clarify the critical person's thoughts, feelings, and needs. Of course, you would fill in the part of the person's criticism that you don't understand, or the part that seems most important to the other person, for the blank lines used in these examples:

- "What is it that bothers you about _____?"

- "Can you be more specific about _____ and tell me how it's bothering you?"

Keep probing and asking questions until you understand what's really bothering the other person and why he or she is being critical. Then either do your best to find a solution to the problem or use clouding to deflect the criticism and end the confrontation. Here's an example:

Critic: You're so selfish. I don't think this relationship will last.

You: What is it that bothers you about our relationship?

Critic: You only care about yourself and your own needs.

You: Can you be more specific about how caring for my own needs bothers you?

Critic: Every night when you come home, you disappear into your office and I don't see you again until it's time for bed.

You: What is it that bothers you about me going into my office when I come home from work?

Critic: You spend all your time in there.

You:	What is it that bothers you about me spending my time in there?
Critic:	It's like we're not even together anymore. I'd like to spend more time with you when you come home.
You:	Okay. I can understand why you're upset. Let's try to work out a compromise so we can spend more time together. (Problem solving)

Or

You:	What is it that bothers you about me spending my time in there?
Critic:	Nothing. You're just a jerk who cares more about his work than you do about me.
You:	You're right. I do care about my work. (Clouding)

ADDITIONAL ASSERTIVENESS TECHNIQUES

So far, you've learned several strategies to help you become more assertive, such as assertive listening and how to deal with criticism. But sometimes special techniques are needed to help you get your needs met. In this section you'll learn four techniques that are very helpful:

1. Broken-record technique

2. Content-to-process shift

3. Momentary delay

4. Time-out

Broken-Record Technique

To put it simply, the broken-record technique means that you say the same thing over and over again—in a nonaggressive way—until you get your needs met. This is especially helpful when you are:

* Saying no to someone

* Setting limits to protect yourself

* Trying to get your needs met with someone who's not being helpful

For example, the broken-record technique could be used to say no to a friend who keeps pestering you with requests for help:

Friend:	I need a ride to the mall today.
You:	Yes, I understand that you need a ride to the mall, but no, I can't help you today.
Friend:	But it's really important that I go today.

You:	Yes, I understand that it's really important to you, but no, I can't help you today.
Friend:	But if I don't go, I'll miss the big sale.
You:	Yes, I understand that you'll miss the big sale, but no, I can't help you today.
Friend:	Okay, fine. I'll go ask someone else.

If you're clear about your position and keep repeating your needs over and over, most people will stop pestering you with their requests.

Similarly, the broken-record technique can be used to make requests of others, for example:

You:	I'd like you to make dinner tonight.
Spouse:	I'm too tired; leave me alone.
You:	I understand you're tired, but I'd still like you to make dinner tonight.
Spouse:	Why are you bothering me? Can't you see I'm watching TV?
You:	Yes, I see you're watching TV, but I'd still like you to make dinner tonight.
Spouse:	What's wrong with you?
You:	There's nothing wrong with me, and I'd like you to make dinner tonight.
Spouse:	Okay. Stop repeating yourself over and over again. I'll make dinner.

Here are some tips for using the broken-record technique:

1. **Be prepared.** Think about what you're going to say or ask for in advance. Write down your request and practice saying it, if necessary. Also, be clear about what you want and don't want. It's fine to begin your request with "I don't want…," but avoid saying, "I can't…," because the other person will simply say, "Of course you can."

2. **Keep it short.** State your needs in one sentence if possible, and don't complicate it with apologies or excuses.

3. **Remain calm.** Use a stress-reduction technique before and after the conversation, if necessary. Continue to remain calm as you firmly restate what you want over and over again, until the person finally gets the message and realizes you won't budge.

4. **Appear confident.** Stand up straight, speak in a clear voice, and maintain good eye contact. And even if you don't feel confident, pretend that you do. Use the old adage, "Fake it till you make it."

5. **Be polite but firm.** It's fine to acknowledge the other person's position and feelings, but don't let those distract you from what you want.

6. **Be persistent.** You'll probably feel awkward repeating yourself, especially if the other person says, "You sound like a broken record," but don't give up. If you don't get what you want

the first time, try again. This simple repetition technique is often successful if you're willing to practice it.

Content-to-Process Shift

This next technique is helpful when a conversation you're having with someone strays far away from the original topic or when the conversation becomes too emotional to carry on with it. When either of these things happen, it's often helpful to shift the focus of the conversation from the content of what's being discussed to the process of how the conversation has shifted. Here are some examples:

- "Excuse me, I want to point out that now we're talking about baseball instead of our problem. Let's get back to what we were discussing earlier."

- "Right now we're both getting upset, and probably we should both cool off before we continue talking. Can we finish discussing this later?"

- "I noticed that you've been very quiet while I've been talking; is there anything you'd like to say?"

- "I'm starting to feel uncomfortable talking about this in a crowded restaurant. Can we continue this conversation when we get home, please?"

When you highlight the content-to-process shift, you're helping both yourself and the other person. You're making sure that the conversation can proceed under the best possible circumstances, and you're also telling the person that you care about what's being discussed. If you ask the other person to postpone the conversation for any reason, make sure you stick to your commitment to continue it in the future.

And, remember, when making any assertive statement like the examples above, make sure your comment is phrased in a nonaggressive way and cannot be taken as an attack. Simply take note of the process of what's happening without making judgments about the other person's character. For example, it would be inappropriate and extremely unhelpful to say, "You jerk, you're just trying to distract me from what's important."

Momentary Delay

It's always okay to take your time when responding to someone's request or comment. It's especially important if you feel confused, overwhelmed, or trapped. If you don't take the time you need to respond to someone in these circumstances, you could easily say something that you'll later regret, or you could make a commitment that you don't want to follow through on.

Taking a momentary delay before responding is helpful because it gives you time to:

1. Think about what's been said and consider your various responses, especially assertive responses

2. Get a better understanding of what the other person has said

3. Focus on your own thoughts and feelings so you can allow them to influence your response, if necessary

Here are some phrases you could use when you need a momentary delay:

- "I'm sorry, could you repeat what you just said? I want to make sure I understand you correctly."

- "So what I hear you saying is [repeat what was said]. Is that correct?"

- "That sounds important. Let me think about that for a minute."

- "I don't think I understood you the first time. Would you mind repeating that?"

- "Could you slowly repeat what you just said? I want to make sure I understand you correctly."

Time-Out

Time-outs can be used in conversations and arguments just the way they're used in football games. Call a time-out in a conversation when you need some extra time to cool down or to think of your response. A typical time-out can last anywhere from one hour to one month—whatever is appropriate to your situation. But if you ask for a time-out, be sure to honor your commitment to get back to the person with a response. Do your best not to use the time-out as a means of avoiding a difficult situation.

Time-outs are appropriate when:

1. The conversation is stuck and neither person knows what to do or say

2. The conversation has taken a nasty turn with name-calling and insults

3. You're feeling angry or upset

4. The other person is getting angry or upset

5. You're feeling pressured to respond and don't know what to do

6. You just want some extra time to think of your response

Typical requests for a time-out include the following:

- "I'll need to get back to you about this [tomorrow, in a week, and so on]."

- "This is important, and I'll need some time to think about it."

- "Time-out. This is getting personal, and I think we both need to take some time to cool off before we discuss this further."

- "I'll need to consult my [spouse, partner, attorney, doctor, and so forth] before making any decisions. I'll get back to you next week."

PUTTING IT ALL TOGETHER

In your effort to become more assertive you've learned many skills in this chapter. So far, you've learned how to:

1. Distinguish assertive actions from passive or aggressive ones

2. Set assertiveness goals

3. Make assertive statements

4. Listen assertively

5. Handle criticism

6. Master additional assertive techniques

Now it's time to put all these skills together and try to reach your assertiveness goals.

Start with Your Least Difficult Goal

When you started this chapter, you ranked your assertiveness goals according to how difficult you thought they would be to achieve. When you're ready to begin, start working on the least difficult goal first, and then after you've achieved it, work your way up. Do not start with your most difficult goal, even if it's the most important. You want to build some successes and a feeling of confidence before you tackle more difficult problems. If you take on a goal that's too hard and you don't succeed, you might become too scared to try being assertive in the future.

Be Prepared

After you've decided which goal you're attempting to reach, review the list of assertive statements you made for that goal—your facts, feelings, and needs. Simply put, this is the script you'll be using when you ask to have your needs met, whether it's asking for something you want, saying no to someone, or setting limits. When you confront the other person, do your best to stick to what you've written and focus on getting your needs met in a nonaggressive way. Also, do your best to anticipate what other skills you might need in this situation, whether it's the broken-record technique, assertive listening, or some other skill you've learned in this chapter.

Also, on your Assertiveness Goals Chart you identified the date you will attempt the assertive communication. Do your best to prepare for it several days in advance and don't let any fear or anxiety that you may feel cause you to avoid it. If your goal requires you to have a scheduled meeting with someone on a certain date, be sure to schedule it a few days in advance. If you'll be talking to a friend or family member, make sure he or she will be available on that day to speak with you. Do everything you can to prepare a successful experience for yourself.

Practice

It's extremely helpful to practice being assertive with someone you trust before trying to meet your goal with the real person involved. Ask a friend to pretend he or she is the person you'll be confronting. Start off by asking the person if now is a good time to talk. Then ask for what you want using your assertive statements. During your practice be sure to allow enough time for the other person to respond. Practice your other assertive skills, too, especially if the other person proves difficult to persuade. Then after you've either received what you want or reached an impasse, ask your friend for feedback. How did you sound? Were you appropriately assertive? Were there any problems? How could you improve? If you reached an impasse in the practice conversation, try using a different assertiveness skill to help you reach your goal. After getting comfortable with this process, ask your friend to become increasingly more difficult to persuade. Or try switching roles. You may learn something valuable from your friend when he or she is pretending to be you.

If you don't have a friend or family member to help you practice, here are some other ideas to help you:

- **Use a mirror.** Stand in front of a mirror and ask for what you want. Then pretend to be the other person involved, too, and respond as you imagine the other person would. Use the same strategies described above and be sure to say the words of your assertive message out loud, rather than just thinking them.

- **Switch places.** Stand on one side of a room or sit in one chair when you're practicing your assertive statements. Then switch to the other side of the room or to another chair when you're pretending to be the person whom you're confronting.

- **Make a recording.** Record what you think the other person will say in response to your assertive statements and then practice making responses.

- **Write a script.** If practicing out loud is too difficult, write a script—or multiple scripts—of how you think the conversation will proceed. Use a simple format, such as "I said,… He or she said,…" Highlight the various techniques that you'll use, such as clouding and time-outs.

Use Your Skills in Real Life

After practicing, it's time to try out your new skills in real life. Of course, the first time you attempt to be assertive, you'll feel nervous. So use a stress-reduction skill from chapter 7 just before engaging in the situation. Remember to breathe, stick to your assertive statements, use your other skills, and just do the best you can. Don't expect the situation to go perfectly. Being assertive takes practice.

Review

After engaging in the assertiveness situation, review what happened by answering the following questions:

- Were you successful?

- If yes, what went right? If no, what went wrong?

- Did you experience any problems that you didn't anticipate?

- If yes, how did you cope with them, or how can you be better prepared in the future?

- On a scale of 1 to 10, how difficult was this situation for you?

- Refer to your original estimate of difficulty on your Assertiveness Goals Chart. Was your estimate accurate? Or was the situation harder or easier than you had anticipated?

- What did you learn about yourself from this situation?

- When will you attempt your next assertiveness goal?

ASSERTIVE COMMUNICATION WORKSHEET

Use the Assertive Communication Worksheet on the following page to help prepare yourself to meet your assertiveness goal and to evaluate the results of your actions.

Assertive Communication Worksheet

BEFORE ENGAGING IN THE ASSERTIVE SITUATION

What is your goal? (Use a nonblaming "I statement.") _____

Date of attempt. (Be as specific as possible.) _____

Predicted difficulty rating (1–10): _____

Make an assertive statement:

- What are the facts? _____
  _____

- What are your feelings? _____
  _____

- What are your needs? _____
  _____

What assertiveness skills do you anticipate using and how will they be helpful?

- Assertive listening: _____
- Acknowledgment: _____
- Clouding: _____
- Probing: _____
- Broken-record technique: _____
- Content-to-process shift: _____
- Momentary delay: _____
- Time-out: _____

How will you rehearse your assertiveness skills? _____

AFTER ENGAGING IN THE ASSERTIVE SITUATION

Did you accomplish your goal? _____
_____

Did you experience any unanticipated problems? _____
_____

Actual difficulty rating (1–10): _____

What did you learn from this experience? _____
_____

When will you attempt your next assertiveness goal? _____

DWIGHT'S ASSERTIVENESS EXAMPLE

Dwight, who struggled with dependent personality disorder, had great difficulty saying no to anyone and setting any limits. This was because he was afraid that if he said no or set limits, he would be abandoned by people, even by his friends. He also thought that he had no right to ask for what he wanted, so when he was around others, he acted very passively and gave in to the needs of others at the expense of his own needs. However, this strategy wasn't particularly helpful because he often felt resentful and sometimes behaved in a very irritated manner, which surprised his friends. Luckily, Dwight was learning about assertiveness skills and had begun to practice them.

The first thing Dwight did was to set his assertiveness goals. One of his goals was "When I see my friend Paul this Saturday night, I want to choose the movie we go to." He rated this goal as a 3 in difficulty, on a scale of 1 to 10, since Paul was such a good friend.

Next he created his assertive statement: "We always go to the movies that you want to see (facts). They're not always movies that I like (feelings). This Saturday I want to choose the movie that we'll see (needs)."

Then Dwight reviewed the various assertiveness skills, such as assertive listening and how to deal with criticism. Afterward he rehearsed the situation in front of a mirror, where he played the roles of both Paul and himself. Finally, he felt prepared to discuss the situation with Paul on Saturday night. Here's what happened:

Dwight: Before we go out tonight I'd like to ask you something.

Paul: Sure, what is it?

Dwight: Well, we always go to the movies that you want to see, but they're not necessarily movies that I like. So tonight, I'd like to choose the movie. (Assertive statement)

Paul: What? You're joking, right?

Dwight: No. I'm not joking. Tonight, I'd like to choose the movie. (Broken-record technique)

Paul: You're being ridiculous. You pick movies to see all the time.

Dwight: It may be that I'm being ridiculous. (Clouding) But I'd still like to pick the movie. (Broken-record technique)

Paul: Come on, let's just drop this. We'll go to the movies and figure something out later. Did you see *American Idol* last night? Who do you think will win this season?

Dwight: Paul, you just changed the subject, and now we're not talking about going to the movies. Can we go back to that? (Content-to-process shift)

Paul: Okay.

Dwight: Is there something that bothers you about me choosing the movie we see? (Probing)

Paul: Well...I've seen the movies you rent.

Dwight: What is it that bothers you about the movies I rent? (Probing)

Paul: You rent a lot of animated films and I don't like animated films. I don't want to start going to animated films on Saturday nights.

Dwight: Okay. So if I don't pick an animated film, can we see something else that I'd like to see? (Problem solving)

Paul: Sure.

Dwight: Thank you.

The next day, Dwight reviewed the situation. His conversation with Paul had been successful. There weren't any problems that Dwight hadn't anticipated and the situation had felt more like a 2 in difficulty, rather than a 3. In addition, Dwight learned that he was capable of being assertive if he prepared and practiced. He also started to believe that he did have the right to ask for his needs to be met, and that his friends wouldn't abandon him. He decided to try another assertiveness goal the following week, and when he tried it, he had similar positive results.

See Dwight's example of completing an Assertive Communication Worksheet on the following page.

Assertive Communication Worksheet—Dwight's Example

BEFORE ENGAGING IN THE ASSERTIVE SITUATION

What is your goal? (Use a nonblaming "I statement.") *When I see my friend Paul this Saturday night, I want to choose the movie we go to.*

Date of attempt. (Be as specific as possible.) *This Saturday, May 15th.*

Predicted difficulty rating (1–10): *3*

Make an assertive statement:

- What are the facts? *We always go to the movies that you want to see.*
- What are your feelings? *They're not always movies that I like.*
- What are your needs? *This Saturday I want to choose the movie that we'll see.*

What assertiveness skills do you anticipate using and how will they be helpful?

- Assertive listening: *I'll use a lot of this to make sure I hear Paul accurately.*
- Acknowledgment: *I don't think Paul will criticize me too much; he's a good friend.*
- Clouding: *I probably won't need clouding.*
- Probing: *I might have to use this to understand Paul's objections.*
- Broken-record technique: *I'll have to repeat myself many times before Paul agrees with me.*
- Content-to-process shift: *I might need this if he tries to change the subject.*
- Momentary delay: *I might need some time to think about what he says.*
- Time-out: *I probably won't need to take a time-out.*

How will you rehearse your assertiveness skills? *I'll rehearse in front of my mirror and play the roles of both Paul and myself.*

AFTER ENGAGING IN THE ASSERTIVE SITUATION

Did you accomplish your goal? *Yes, Paul agreed to see a movie that I like, as long as it wasn't animated.*

Did you experience any unanticipated problems? *Paul accused me of being ridiculous, so I had to use some clouding, and I had to stop him from changing the subject. But besides that, I felt well prepared.*

Actual difficulty rating (1–10): *2*

What did you learn from this experience? *I can get my needs met sometimes and be assertive, if I'm prepared and I rehearse.*

When will you attempt your next assertiveness goal? *Next weekend I'll ask my neighbor Laura to return the garden hose that she borrowed several months ago.*

IN CONCLUSION

As you can see from Dwight's example, assertive communication skills take dedication and practice to learn. However, they are essential to establishing healthy relationships and getting your needs met in an appropriate way, even though few people are ever taught these skills. Right now, you're lucky enough to learn them. So if you recognize that you rely on passive or aggressive communication styles, dedicate the next few weeks or months to learning these skills, and you'll be grateful for the rest of your life.

CHAPTER 10

Learn Coping Imagery

Coping imagery is an easy-to-learn technique that will help you to complete difficult tasks with added confidence, especially tasks that you've been avoiding because of excessive anxiety. As its name implies, coping imagery uses your ability to visualize images in your mind's eye in order to deal with stressful situations. If you frequently daydream or lose track of time while reading a good book, you probably have a good imagination that allows you to create stories and pictures in your thoughts. This is the same type of imagery that you'll be using with this technique. If you're a person who has not got a vivid imagination, this technique can still be helpful, but it might require additional practice. In fact, if you do have trouble using your imagination, you might prepare yourself by simply daydreaming about yourself in a variety of situations.

USING COPING IMAGERY

When you use this technique, you'll identify the various steps of a task and highlight those that are the most difficult. Then you'll learn how to manage those steps by using stress-reduction techniques, coping thoughts, and visualization before you engage in the task in real life.

Here's an example of a good use of coping imagery. Ava, who struggled with avoidant personality disorder, regularly refused to join her coworkers for Friday night happy hour at a nearby restaurant because she was afraid that she might embarrass herself in front of them and eventually be rejected. However, she had already experienced some success using the stress-reduction techniques and relaxation skills that she had learned to do (see chapter 7). So finally, one day she accepted her coworkers' invitation, despite how scared the upcoming event made her feel. To give herself more confidence, Ava decided to use coping imagery.

Several days before the event, she began the process of identifying the steps involved in the task, such as leaving work, getting to the restaurant, and talking to people. Then she identified which step made her feel the most anxious, and she recognized that the thought of starting up a conversation was the most stressful. Next she used cue-controlled relaxation and several coping statements to help her deal with that specific stressor. Her coping statements included thoughts like "I don't have to do it perfectly; I just have to be friendly." Then she imagined herself going through the entire evening successfully using her new coping skills. And finally, on the day of the event she felt confident enough to test her new skills in real life.

The six steps for using coping imagery are the following:

1. Learn to relax.

2. Identify the steps of your task.

3. Identify the stressors.

4. Plan coping strategies.

5. Rehearse coping strategies.

6. Apply your coping strategies to real life.

The technique for using coping imagery was created by Arthur Freeman and his associates. It is discussed in their book *Clinical Applications of Cognitive Therapy*.[69] And many of the suggestions used here were adapted from the book *Thoughts and Feelings*.[57]

Step 1: Learn to Relax

Hopefully, you've been practicing the stress-reduction and relaxation techniques from chapter 7 and have found several that are helpful. Ideally, you should be using some of the faster techniques with some success, such as cue-controlled relaxation and mindful breathing. If you haven't been practicing these techniques, you should review those skills and practice them before proceeding to step 4 in this chapter. To complete your mastery of coping imagery, you'll need a technique that helps you to relax during stressful situations.

Step 2: Identify the Steps of Your Task

In order to help yourself successfully complete a difficult task, it's first necessary to identify the various steps of that task from the beginning to the end, so that you can see where the problems will arise. To begin, pick a task that you've been avoiding, one that makes you anxious or one that just seems very difficult to accomplish. It could be something that you have to do, like give a presentation at work, or something that you'd like to do, such as to ask a friend for a favor or, as in Ava's case, to socialize with some coworkers after work. If you have several difficult tasks you'd like to accomplish, rank them in their order of difficulty and start with the easiest one. This will give you time to practice the technique and to build your self-confidence.

Next, describe as many steps of the task as you can using either a narrative form or an outline. Do your best to describe the scene using the present tense as if it were happening right now; doing this will help you in step 3. For example, narrative form looks like this: "First, I ask to borrow the car in the morning and I start to feel anxious. Later, I back out of the driveway and I notice the butterflies in my stomach. I drive all the way down to the store on State and Main. I have to drive around looking for a parking spot, which makes me angry. Then I go into the store to buy a shirt. I'm anxious and I hope no one asks to help me. Finally, I drive home feeling nervous about the shirt I bought."

Or you can simply outline the event and order the steps like this: "(1) Ask to borrow the car—anxious thoughts begin. (2) Later, back out of the driveway—probably experience butterflies in my stomach. (3) Drive to store on State and Main. (4) Drive around looking for a parking spot—feel angry. (5) Go into store and buy a shirt—feel anxious that someone will ask to help me. (6) Drive home feeling nervous." The narrative form is more detailed and is the preferred method; however, if you don't have time, the outline method is acceptable.

Whichever method you choose, be as detailed as possible. Also, be sure to include the difficult events that happen before the task starts, such as "Ask to borrow the car in the morning," because people's anxiety levels often heighten long before they actually begin a task. Then describe what you need to do when the task starts and what you need to do when it concludes. In order to fully prepare yourself, write one conclusion that ends positively and one that ends negatively. (See Ava's example in step 3.)

Be as specific and detailed as possible when identifying your steps. Throughout your description, do your best to identify:

- The steps that are most difficult

- Anxious emotions you expect to have

- Anxiety-provoking thoughts you expect to have

- Any anxious physical reactions you expect to have, such as butterflies in your stomach, headaches, muscle tension, sweaty palms, rapid breathing, light-headedness, pounding heartbeat, and so on

- The steps where you expect to feel out of control or helpless

Step 3: Identify the Stressors

Hopefully, you've already identified several difficult steps in your task. But to fully prepare for this situation, you should imagine yourself engaging in the task while paying attention to your reactions. The steps that make you feel especially anxious are the stressors that will require the use of special coping skills.

In order to imagine yourself in the situation, you can use one of the techniques described below, such as making a recording of your narrative. Then find a time and place where you can listen to your recording without any interruptions. Close your eyes, relax as best you can, and try to imagine yourself doing all of the steps in your task. Use your imaginary senses to help you stay focused. See yourself in the location where the event will take place and notice the people who will be there with you. Try to imagine any sounds or smells that might be present in the scene. Do your best to notice as many sensory details as possible and imagine yourself completing each step of the task.

As you imagine yourself completing each step, pay attention to any anxious reactions you experience, including your thoughts, your feelings, and your physical reactions. Make a mental note to yourself where they occurred, and after you've finished imagining the entire task, mark these stressors on your narrative or outline. Later, when you rehearse the task in step 5, and when you complete the task in real life step 6, these will be the places where you'll use your special coping strategies.

Here are three techniques that will help you to imagine yourself doing the task:

1. Record your narrative or outline. Use a tape recorder, an MP3 player, or a video camera. Record yourself describing the task and pause after each step to allow yourself time to fully imagine the scene.

2. Read your narrative or outline and pause after each step for self-reflection. Take your time to fully imagine yourself completing each step and to notice all of your reactions. Then read the next step.

3. Have a friend read your narrative or outline to you. Ask your friend to pause after each step and, again, note all of your reactions.

AVA'S EXAMPLE

Here are the steps that Ava described for her task of going out for a social evening with her coworkers. She first wrote it out as a narrative and then recorded it on her iPod so that she could listen to it. Ava imagined herself completing each step in the future and underlined the stressors that made her feel especially anxious.

On Thursday I start to anticipate what will happen on Friday. I know that Sandra will ask me to go out with her and everybody else after work. Then on Friday, around noon, <u>Sandra asks me to join them at the restaurant for drinks. I feel very, very nervous but say yes.</u> Around 4:30, just before work ends, I feel scared. <u>I have thoughts like, "I should just back out" and "What did I get myself into?"</u> Around 5:00, I see everyone collecting their jackets and my fear becomes very strong. <u>I feel tingling in my hands.</u> I get my jacket too and then follow them into the elevator. There are people coming with us whom I've never spoken to before. <u>They're all talking about their weekends and I don't know what to say. I continue to feel anxious.</u> Some of the people are looking at me. When we get downstairs, people start gathering in groups. I don't know which group to go with. I walk down the street tagging behind them all to the restaurant, and once we get in, I don't know which person I should sit next to. <u>I'm scared and I start to think, "What if I sit next to someone who doesn't like me?"</u> Eventually, I sit next to someone and <u>I'm stuck in a corner where I can't get out very easily.</u> When the waitress comes, I don't know what to order, so I just ask for a Coke. I notice other people looking at me and think, "Maybe they're wondering if I have an alcohol problem." <u>Then I sit there waiting for someone to talk to me and I think about what I might say. I'm really worried about saying the wrong thing to someone.</u> Eventually, someone asks me what I'm doing this weekend and I tell her that I don't have any plans. <u>I wonder if she thinks that I'm boring for not having any friends to do anything with.</u> I ask her what she's doing this weekend and she tells me her plans.

Negative Conclusion: For the rest of the night I sit there silently by myself. I listen to other people having conversations. <u>Barely anyone notices that I'm even there.</u> Then when everyone decides to leave, no one says goodbye to me and <u>I go home by myself on the bus.</u>

Positive Conclusion: Eventually, someone sits next to me and starts a conversation. Then Sandra comes over and joins in the conversation. I don't say much but I feel included. When the evening is over, Sandra thanks me for coming and offers to drive me home.

Notice that Ava recorded two possible conclusions to her task, one that ends negatively and one that ends positively. This allows her to prepare for both scenarios. Try doing this yourself when you prepare your own series of steps.

Step 4: Plan Coping Strategies

As you probably noticed from Ava's example, as well as from your own narrative, there are several stressors involved in this task; it's not just one big stressor. Ava anticipates having several worrisome thoughts and nervous physical sensations. As Matthew McKay and his colleagues point out, identifying these smaller stressors helps to "demystify" the source of your anxiety.[57] Many people avoid getting into a situation or doing a task because it makes them feel anxious or afraid in a generalized fashion, but they never really think about the specific parts that make them feel that way. And rather than coping with those individual parts, they avoid the entire task. Making the distinction between one big stressor and several smaller ones is important, because it's usually easier to prepare for and to cope with several smaller stressors rather than the big one, which can appear to be overwhelming.

Also notice that Ava's anxiety about the task is experienced as thoughts, physical feelings, and emotions, not just as emotions alone. You'll probably experience the same things, so you'll need to prepare both a stress-reduction skill and a coping statement to deal with each stressor. Then in step 5 you'll rehearse these coping strategies. Once again, you'll listen to your narrative or outline, but this time when you encounter a stressor, you'll also use a stress-reduction technique and a coping statement to deal with your anxiety.

STRESS-REDUCTION AND RELAXATION SKILLS

As mentioned in step 1, you'll need to master one of the stress-reduction and relaxation skills in order to handle your task. Two that are highly recommended are cue-controlled relaxation and mindful breathing. Both of these can help you to quickly relax and cope with distressing emotions and physical sensations. Review chapter 7 for instructions on how to use one or both of these skills.

COPING STATEMENTS

In chapter 5, you practiced challenging your automatic thoughts using alternative, balanced thoughts. You can use the same process here when you encounter distressing thoughts in your narrative or outline. You can consider the experiences that both strengthen and weaken that thought and then create a healthier, more balanced thought. Then you can use this as your coping thought when you rehearse the task.

Similarly, in chapter 4, you learned how to use coping statements. You can use any of those that were helpful, or you can create new coping statements that will help you deal with your task. In general, coping statements *erase* stress and anxiety by helping you do the following:

- **E**mphasize your coping plan and specific coping strategies. (For example, "I just have to stay focused as best I can and use my assertive communication skills.")

- **R**elax. (For example, "If I just relax and breathe, I can get through this.")

- **A**ccept what's happening without panicking. (For example, "My feelings make me uncomfortable right now, but I can accept them without panicking.")

- **S**top your catastrophic thoughts and fears. (For example, "My thoughts don't control my life; I do.")

- **E**ase unreasonably high expectations. (For example, "I'll just do the best I can; it doesn't have to be perfect.")

Here are some additional coping statements that you can use.[57] Mark those that are helpful to you or use them for inspiration to create your own coping statements that will help you deal with your specific task:

- "This situation won't last forever."

- "I've already been through many other painful experiences, and I've always survived."

- "This too shall pass."

- "I can be anxious and still deal with the situation."

- "I'm strong enough to handle what's happening to me right now."

- "This is an opportunity for me to learn how to cope with my anxiety."

- "I can ride this out and not let it get to me."

- "I can take all the time I need right now to let go and relax."

- "I've survived other situations like this before, and I'll survive this one too."

- "My anxiety [fear, sadness, and so on] won't kill me; it just doesn't feel good right now."

- "These are just my feelings, and eventually they'll change and go away."

- "It's okay to feel sad [anxious, afraid, sad, and so on] sometimes."

- "I can think different thoughts if I want to."

- "I'm not in any danger right now."

- "So what?"

- "This situation is difficult, but it's only temporary."

- "I'm strong and I can deal with this."

AVA'S EXAMPLE

For each stressor in her narrative, Ava identified at least one coping statement that she could use in addition to using either cue-controlled relaxation or mindful breathing. Here are several examples:

- *Sandra asks me to join them... I feel very, very nervous but say yes.*

  "Just focus on my mindful breathing and relax. Slow breath in, slow breath out."

- *I have thoughts like "I should just back out" and "What did I get myself into?"*

  "I shouldn't just back out. I've handled scary situations like this before, and I can handle this one too."

- *I feel tingling in my hands.*

   "This situation won't last forever, and eventually I'll feel relaxed."

- *I sit there waiting for someone to talk to me and think about what to say.*

   "I can relax using cue-controlled relaxation to release any tension."

- *I wonder if that person thinks I'm boring…*

   "So what? I don't have to be perfect; I'm doing the best I can."

Step 5: Rehearse Coping Strategies

Once you've identified at least one coping statement for each stressor, you can begin rehearsing your coping strategies. First, rewrite your narrative or outline. Insert a coping statement and a reminder to use either cue-controlled relaxation or mindful breathing after each stressor. Then either rerecord your new format, read it through again, or ask someone to read it to you. And remember to give yourself plenty of time after each stressor to relax and use your coping thoughts.

Here's the beginning of Ava's coping script, with her coping actions in parentheses:

On Thursday I start to anticipate what will happen on Friday. I know that Sandra will ask me to go out with her and everybody else after work. Then on Friday, around noon, <u>Sandra asks me to join them at the restaurant for drinks. I feel very, very nervous but say yes.</u> (Use mindful breathing. Coping thought: "Just focus on my mindful breathing and relax. Slow breath in, slow breath out.") *Around 4:30, just before work ends, I feel scared. <u>I have thoughts like "I should just back out" and "What did I get myself into?"</u>* (Continue to use mindful breathing. Coping thought: "I shouldn't just back out. I've handled scary situations like this before, and I can handle this one too.") *Around 5:00, I see everyone collecting their jackets and my fear becomes very strong. <u>I feel tingling in my hands.</u>* (Use cue-controlled relaxation. Coping thought: "This situation won't last forever, and eventually I'll feel relaxed.") *I get my jacket too and then follow them into the elevator. There are people coming with us whom I've never spoken to before. <u>They're all talking about their weekends and I don't know what to say. I continue to feel anxious.</u>* (Continue to use mindful breathing. Coping thought: "I don't have to be perfect; this feeling will soon pass.")

As you listen to your narrative or outline again and begin using your coping skills in your imagination, keep track of your anxiety levels. You can use a scale of 0 to 10, with 0 meaning no anxiety and 10 meaning the worst anxiety you've ever experienced. During your rehearsals, notice where your anxiety peaks, and then keep repeating your rehearsals until your anxiety falls to a comfortable level, usually around 4 on the scale. It's unlikely that your anxiety will disappear completely, but you should be able to recognize that your anxiety diminishes in intensity as you use your coping skills. And remember, this process will take multiple practice sessions to be effective. Continue to rehearse your stress-reduction relaxation skills and coping statements in your imagination until you feel ready and confident to test your skills in real life.

If your rehearsals do not reduce your anxiety or they don't make you feel more confident, reassess your coping statements. Maybe one or even several of them need to be revised. Also, try using a different stress-reduction technique. For example, if you've been using cue-controlled relaxation, try mindful breathing instead and vice versa.

Step 6: Apply Your Coping Strategies to Real Life

Once you're able to successfully reduce your anxiety level for each stressor during rehearsal, you're ready to tackle your task in real life. Of course, in real life the task will probably include variables that you hadn't prepared for, such as the way another person reacts, but don't panic. Just remember to continue using the coping statements and relaxation techniques that helped you in rehearsal as best you can. Write them down and keep them with you, for reminders and for support. When you take on the real situation, you might not be able to say your coping statements out loud, but you can certainly think the words to yourself to ease your anxiety and bolster your confidence. Similarly, you might not be able to close your eyes and use mindful breathing after feeling each stressor, but you can certainly breathe mindfully with your eyes open and help yourself to relax.

Do the best you can, especially when you use coping imagery for the first time in a real-life situation. The task might not go as perfectly as it did when you rehearsed it, but nothing ever does. To increase your chances of success in the future, continue to practice this technique, especially if you have several tasks that you'd like to accomplish. Start with the easiest task first and work your way up in difficulty so you can build your self-confidence.

IN CONCLUSION

Coping imagery is a quick and helpful technique to help you deal with difficult tasks that cause anxiety and avoidance. However, like every other technique in this workbook, coping imagery requires some practice. So when you begin using coping imagery, give yourself several days to prepare for the event before using the technique in real life. This will increase your chances of successfully completing the task with self-confidence and skill.

Also note that coping imagery is not effective for every problem. If you try this technique and it doesn't work or if you experience excessive fear about something, like being alone or making mistakes, you might getter better results using the stress-inoculation technique discussed in chapter 11.

Use Exposure to Confront Feared Situations and Emotions

Exposure is a treatment that helps you to confront situations that cause fear, anxiety, and avoidance. Exposure treatment is effective because it is based on a very important psychological principle: if you remain in contact with an anxiety-provoking situation for a long enough period of time, your level of anxiety will decrease naturally.

However, let's be clear that this applies only to situations that are not life threatening. When using exposure, you should never put your life in danger.

WHY AVOIDANCE DOESN'T WORK

Unfortunately, many people with personality disorders completely avoid anxiety-provoking situations, which only increases their levels of anxiety and avoidance in the future. Here's what happens:

1. They encounter something that scares them, such as an opportunity to try something new.

2. They have self-critical thoughts, such as "I can't handle this situation. It will overwhelm me."

3. They notice physical sensations related to anxiety, such as shortness of breath, increased heart rate, and muscle tension.

4. They avoid or flee the situation instead of dealing with it.

5. Their level of anxiety and their physical tension then quickly decrease.

6. They continue to believe that they can't handle the situation when it occurs again at some future date, and they continue to avoid all similar situations.

Unfortunately, avoidance often appears to be a good strategy for reducing your anxiety level. However, in the future you'll continue being scared of any similar types of situations unless you learn how to confront them and cope with them. This is where exposure can be especially helpful.

WHY EXPOSURE IS HELPFUL

It might sound intimidating to remain in contact with something you're afraid of, but the type of exposure discussed in this chapter is performed in a very gradual manner.

In this chapter, you'll learn two types of exposure-based treatments:

1. Stress inoculation, to help you confront anxiety-provoking situations

2. Emotion exposure, to help you confront distressing emotions

Stress inoculation, created by psychologist Donald Meichenbaum,[70] will teach you how to create a graded list of fearful experiences called a *hierarchy* so that you can start confronting your least fearful experiences before working up to your more difficult ones. You'll also learn to relax, use coping statements, and imagine yourself dealing with the situations that frighten you before confronting them in real life.

Similarly, *emotion exposure* will help you learn to tolerate uncomfortable or distressing emotions that many people try to avoid. Note that this technique is frequently used in dialectical behavior therapy to treat people who are struggling with borderline personality disorder.[14]

Exposure is also used to treat other mental health problems, such as phobias, panic disorder, and obsessive-compulsive disorder (which is different than obsessive-compulsive personality disorder). The procedure described in this chapter is very similar to the exposure treatment used for these other problems, but this chapter will focus on treating avoidance issues related to personality disorders. If you're also struggling with one of the above-named problems, you could try using this form of exposure, but you might be better served if you were to seek the guidance of a mental health professional who specializes in your problem, or if you consulted other books, such as Edmund Bourne's *The Anxiety and Phobia Workbook*[71] and Matthew McKay, Martha Davis, and Patrick Fanning's *Thoughts & Feelings*,[57] from which some of this material has been adapted.

STRESS INOCULATION

If you used coping imagery while working with chapter 10, you've already used one form of exposure. Coping imagery helps you to confront difficult tasks by first identifying the various steps required for the task and then rehearsing your coping strategies in your imagination. This rehearsal is a type of exposure treatment. Sometimes, however, you might not know what the steps of a difficult task will be or you might be too afraid to confront the task at all.

In these cases, it might be hard to prepare for the situation using coping imagery. Instead, you'll need to use a type of exposure called stress inoculation. Stress inoculation uses many of the same skills as coping imagery, but there are a few important differences, such as building a hierarchy of fearful experiences and closely monitoring your anxiety level during visualization. For people struggling with personality disorders, stress inoculation can be used to cope with situations such as these:

- Setting boundaries, disagreeing, and saying no when necessary

- Asking someone for help

- Tolerating mistakes (yours and others)

- Tolerating lapses in your strict set of principles and values

- Loosening your control of projects or activities

- Getting rid of unneeded or worthless objects

- Caring for yourself with little or no help from others

- Making decisions and doing tasks with little or no help from others

- Interacting with people in a new way, such as not trying to please them all the time

- Engaging in social situations in a new way, such as spending more time with the people you know

- Dealing with difficult relationships, such as ending them when necessary

- Practicing how to trust and forgive people, such as sharing information about yourself

- Trying out new activities, like hobbies, recreational activities, and traveling

- Performing tasks in a new way, such as meeting deadlines in a timely manner, instead of procrastinating

Notice that all of these examples require you to do something in a new way. Even trusting and forgiving people requires you to treat them in a new way, such as sharing information about yourself. In order for stress inoculation to work and for your life to improve, you'll need to practice new ways of behaving.

THE SIX STEPS OF STRESS INOCULATION

Here are the six steps of stress inoculation:

1. Practice relaxation skills.

2. Choose a fear to confront.

3. Build an exposure hierarchy.

4. Develop your coping statements.

5. Begin stress inoculation.

6. Engage in real-life exposure.

If you've been using some of the stress-reduction and relaxation skills found in chapter 7 and you've already tried coping imagery from chapter 10, stress inoculation will be an easy skill for you to learn.

Otherwise, you'll need to refer to those chapters to review some skill components, such as developing a coping statement, but you'll be directed to those skills throughout this chapter.

Before actually beginning to use the procedure described below, read through the entire description so that you're familiar with and understand all of the steps involved.

Step 1: Practice Relaxation Skills

There are four relaxation skills you'll need to use that are discussed in chapter 7. They are progressive muscle relaxation, cue-controlled relaxation, mindful breathing, and safe-place visualization. If you've been practicing these and have found them effective, you're ready to begin stress inoculation. Otherwise, you should return to chapter 7 and practice those skills before continuing. They should lower your stress and tension to a comfortable level and make you feel confident enough to take on some challenging situations.

Step 2: Choose a Fear to Confront

For some people, choosing a fear to confront may be easy. You might be able to identify it right away. For example, you might say, "Yes, I'm afraid of making mistakes." Or you may have several fears that you'd like to confront; for example, "I'm afraid of making mistakes, asking for help, and trying new activities." If so, pick one that you'd like to focus on, maybe one that seems easiest or the one that most interferes with your life, and then move on to step 3.

Some other people, however, may have trouble identifying their fears. As stated previously, people with personality disorders struggle with old, inflexible ways of thinking, and this can sometimes make it hard for them to identify their fears. They might say, "That's the way I am and I can't change." If you're having trouble identifying a fear to confront, try one of the following suggestions.

First, if you've already done the work of identifying your negative core beliefs in chapter 6, go back and see if there's something there that you're afraid of. Take your negative core belief and restate it as a fear. Ask yourself why your belief is so frightening. For example, if your core belief is "I'm incapable of doing anything by myself," your fear might be "I'm afraid to do anything by myself because I'll mess it up so completely that other people will laugh at me." Or if your belief is "I'm defective," your fear might be "I'm afraid to let others get close enough to me to see my defects, because then they might leave me." Be honest with yourself. Nothing in your life can improve if you're not honest about your fears.

Second, if you're still having trouble identifying a fear to confront, ask yourself this question, "What would I like to be doing in my life that I'm not doing now?" Some answers might be creating healthier relationships, finding a new job, trying something new, or anything else. Then ask yourself, "What's the thought that's holding me back and preventing me from doing that?" Finally, rephrase that thought as a statement that can be challenged, using the phrase: "I'm afraid of…" For example, you might say, "I'd like to interact with people in a new way. I'd like to be more open with them." But the thought that's holding you back may be, "If I'm more open with other people, I'll say something that will embarrass me, and I'll never get over it." So your fear might be stated as, "I'm afraid of being open with people and embarrassing myself."

Do your best to state your fear as something specific that can be challenged in a series of steps. For example, if you simply state your fear as "I'm afraid I'm defective," it might be hard to challenge it with a series of steps. In this case, you'd have to create several scenarios that would generally make you feel defective. However, if you could identify more details about what it is that makes you feel defective—details that specifically address "when," "why," and "what makes you feel this way?"—then you could create more specific ways to challenge your fear. For example, it's easier to think of ways to challenge this fear because it's more specific: "I'm afraid to let others get close to me and see my defects, because then they might leave me." To challenge this statement, you could create several scenarios in which you do things imperfectly, say things imperfectly, or reveal your character flaws to others just to see what their reactions would be. Then you could use your coping skills to deal with these situations and, over time, you would begin to see your anxiety level decrease.

Step 3: Build an Exposure Hierarchy

To conquer your fear, you'll need to purposely confront it in order to learn how to cope with its challenges. However, this should be done gradually, in a way that allows you to confront easier situations before you move on to more difficult ones. Therefore, the next step of this process is to make a hierarchy, or a graded list, of related situations that cause you to feel fear and anxiety. You should list ten to twenty situations that challenge your fear. Make sure that they range in difficulty from easier to harder or from low anxiety to high anxiety.

The purpose of building a hierarchy is to allow you to confront your least anxiety-provoking situations before you take on the task of confronting situations that might set off greater anxiety for you. For example, Olivia struggled with obsessive-compulsive personality disorder. In step 2 she identified her fear as, "I'm afraid of mistakes being made at work, at home, and in public, by me and by others." Olivia also recognized that she experienced mild distress when she made mistakes at home, moderate distress when she made mistakes at work, and severe distress when she made mistakes in public. So when she built her hierarchy of challenges, she began using stress inoculation at home before applying it to anxiety-provoking situations at work and in public.

CREATE YOUR HIERARCHY USING THESE FOUR VARIABLES

If you can think of ten to twenty situations that challenge your fear and that range in difficulty from easier to harder, write them down on a piece of paper in the order of their difficulty. When you've done that, you're ready to begin. However, most people need some help with creating a broad range of challenges. To help you design your hierarchy, here are four variables that you can manipulate to create different levels of difficulty. These variables are as follows:

1. **How close you are to your feared experience.** As a rule, the closer you are, the more fear you'll experience. For example, if you are afraid of trying new activities and you want to try dancing, your first step might be to sit in your car outside of the dance studio, your second step might be to walk past the door of the studio, your third step might be to enter the dance studio and ask for information, and so on, until you arrive on the dance floor.

2. **How much time you spend in contact with your feared experience.** Usually, the more time you think you'll have to spend in contact, the more fear you'll experience. For example, if you are afraid of social situations, your first step might be to spend five minutes in the

lunchroom with your coworkers, your second step might be to spend ten minutes at an after-work gathering, your third step might be to spend fifteen minutes at a party, and so on.

3. **How fearful each step is.** For example, if you are afraid to trust people because you're afraid they might hurt you, you could start with people who are closer to you before trusting individuals you don't know so well. In this case, you might start by trusting someone like a parent or a sibling, then try trusting a friend, and, finally, trust an acquaintance, such as a coworker.

4. **How much support you receive during the feared event.** Usually, tasks are easier if you have someone with you to provide emotional support. For example, if you are afraid of getting rid of things, such as old newspapers and found objects that clutter your home, you might start by asking a friend to help you. Then you might progress to just having a friend stand nearby to offer support. And, finally, you might just ask a friend to be available by phone if you should need his or her support.

CREATE A RANGE OF CHALLENGING SITUATIONS

At this point, you should have recorded ten to twenty situations that challenge your fear, ranging in difficulty from easy to hard. However, if you are still having trouble creating your hierarchy, imagine the easiest situation and then the most difficult. Put those two at opposite ends of the hierarchy and then use some of the recommendations listed above to fill in the rest of the steps. For example:

- Break your task into separate, smaller steps, as in the example above of learning how to dance.

- Divide the task into ever-increasing increments of time, as in the example above of spending more time in social situations.

- Break your task into steps that include multiple forms of support from people you trust, as in the example above of asking for help.

After you've completed your hierarchy, make sure that it increases in difficulty in a consistent way. For example, if step 5 seems much more difficult than step 4, create a step in the middle. Remember, the purpose of this exercise is to help you reach your goals and to help you build your confidence to take on more difficult situations. Do your best to help yourself succeed.

PLAN FOR SITUATIONS THAT WILL OCCUR IN THE NEAR FUTURE

When creating your hierarchy, pick situations that you can set up easily in the near future. This means picking situations over which you can exercise some control or picking events that you are reasonably certain will happen. For example, if you're afraid of trying new activities, create a hierarchy that includes only activities you can attempt in the near future. If you were to include scuba diving but you have no access to this activity, you'd be stuck. Similarly, if one of your activities is to talk to someone you don't expect to see for the next ten months, you'd also be stuck. Ideally, you should create a hierarchy of events that you can attempt in the next four to eight weeks.

PREPARE FOR REAL-LIFE SITUATIONS

Finally, while creating your hierarchy, keep in mind that these are situations you'll want to attempt in real life, too, after you've rehearsed them in your imagination. Therefore, don't put anything on your hierarchy that you can't try to do in real life. For example, if you are afraid of social situations and you want a friend to help you, don't pick someone who can't really do it, such as a person who lives too far away or is ill. Imagine being supported by someone who is truly available and would be willing to help.

EXAMPLES OF HIERARCHIES

Here are three examples of hierarchies for you to think about while you are creating your own. The lower-numbered difficulty rankings represent the easier tasks that cause less anxiety. The higher-numbered rankings represent more difficult tasks that cause greater anxiety.

Example: Olivia—Obsessive-Compulsive Personality Disorder

Fear: "Mistakes being made at home, at the office, and in public."

Difficulty Ranking	Scene
1	*Let Carl [her husband] take out the garbage, whether or not he forgets.*
2	*Allow kids or Carl to do the dishes without me checking to see how clean they are.*
3	*Allow Carl to do the laundry.*
4	*Allow kids to do homework by themselves without my supervision.*
5	*Allow Carl or kids to vacuum the house.*
6	*Ask boss for clarification on what he wants me to do in the afternoon only two times.*
7	*Ask boss for clarification on what he wants me to do in the afternoon only once.*
8	*Do afternoon tasks without asking boss for any clarification.*
9	*At work, turn in my team's financial report after I spend only one hour reviewing it.*
10	*Turn in team's report after I spend only thirty minutes reviewing it.*
11	*Let another team member review our report and turn it in without doing any review myself.*
12	*Leave work at 5:30 p.m., even if my work isn't complete.*
13	*Leave work with everyone else at 5:00 p.m., even if my work isn't complete.*
14	*Allow Carl to order food for the whole family at McDonald's.*
15	*Allow Carl to order food for the whole family at a nice restaurant.*
16	*Go out to dinner wearing clothes that are noticeably dirty and stained.*

Example: Patrick—Paranoid Personality Disorder

Fear: "Trusting others."

Difficulty Ranking	Scene
1	Tell my mother about my vacation plans.
2	Tell my brother about my vacation plans.
3	Offer to let my brother borrow my car next weekend.
4	Tell the woman at the corner market what my real first name is the next time I go in.
5	Go to a new market and give the clerk my first name.
6	Talk to the telemarketer the next time one calls—most likely this week.
7	Create an e-mail account using my real name.
8	Sign up for an online Facebook account using fake personal information.
9	Tell a stranger on the bus what my real full name is.
10	Buy something small online using a PayPal account.
11	Buy something online using my credit card.
12	Sign up for an online Facebook account using my real information.
13	Put my mail in the garbage without shredding it (provided it doesn't have my social security number or bank account number on it).
14	Keep my window shades open while I'm home in the daytime.
15	Keep my window shades open while I'm home at night.

Example: Hillary—Histrionic Personality Disorder	
Fear: "Other people won't like me if I'm not interesting or trying to impress them."	
Difficulty Ranking	Scene
1	*Don't talk to anyone on the train while commuting to work.*
2	*Don't try to act amusing at the weekly Friday morning meeting.*
3	*Don't flirt with John at work.*
4	*Go out after work with friends and don't offer my opinions about anything they're talking about, unless someone asks.*
5	*Offer to let Jennifer run the Tuesday lunch meeting.*
6	*Wear plain, unattractive clothes to work one day.*
7	*Wear plain, unattractive clothes and no makeup to work one day.*
8	*Go to the bar with Kim in plain, simple clothing and no makeup one evening.*
9	*Go to the bar alone in plain, simple clothing and no makeup one evening.*
10	*Confess to John that I don't understand some of his jokes instead of pretending I do understand and laughing.*

Now create your own hierarchy of ten to twenty events using the examples and suggestions above and using the blank Hierarchy List that follows step 4. Be sure to rank your tasks in the order of their difficulty.

Step 4: Develop Your Coping Statements

When confronting difficult situations, coping statements are very important. Coping statements are thoughts that provide you with motivation, inspiration, and reminders that you are strong enough and capable enough to take on challenges that you've previously avoided. For each situation in your Hierarchy List, you should create one or two coping statements that will help you deal with your anxiety, especially reminders to relax physically.

Here's a tip from Matthew McKay, Martha Davis, and Patrick Fanning about how to create helpful coping thoughts.[57] Visualize yourself taking on each situation, one at a time. As you do this, pay attention to your anxious thoughts and physical feelings. Then create a coping statement to respond to those thoughts and feelings. For example, your coping statement might include:

- Your plan to handle the situation, especially if it becomes very difficult ("I'll use mindful breathing to help me relax")

- How likely it is that the worst will happen ("It's very unlikely that this person will yell at me; he might just become upset")

- The length of time that your anxiety will last ("This situation is difficult, but it won't last longer than a few minutes")

- Reminders of other coping skills you can use ("If the situation gets very difficult, I can use my assertive communication skills")

For more examples of coping statements and suggestions on how to develop your own, review the sections on coping statements in chapters 4 and 10. Then use the blank Hierarchy List that follows Olivia's example to record one or two coping thoughts for each of the situations on your hierarchy. Here are some examples from Olivia's Coping Statements.

<table>
<tr><th colspan="3">Example—Olivia's Coping Statements</th></tr>
<tr><td colspan="3">Fear: Mistakes being made at home, at the office, and in public.</td></tr>
<tr><th>Difficulty Ranking</th><th>Scene</th><th>Coping Statement(s)</th></tr>
<tr><td>2</td><td>Allow kids or Carl to do the dishes without me checking to see how clean they are.</td><td>Even if they're not 100 percent clean, it's very unlikely that anything will happen because of it.
I'll just do my best to breathe and relax.</td></tr>
<tr><td>7</td><td>Ask boss for clarification on what he wants me to do in the afternoon only once.</td><td>Just relax as best I can. My boss has expressed a lot of confidence in my work and a desire for me to work independently.</td></tr>
<tr><td>10</td><td>Turn in team's report after I spend only thirty minutes reviewing it.</td><td>The reports they write are frequently excellent.
I'll spend ten minutes breathing and relaxing after I turn it in.</td></tr>
<tr><td>12</td><td>Leave work at 5:30 p.m., even if my work isn't complete.</td><td>I don't have to be perfect all the time.
I can use mindful breathing during the car ride home to help me relax.</td></tr>
<tr><td>16</td><td>Go out to dinner wearing clothes that are noticeably dirty and stained.</td><td>I can feel uncomfortable for two hours; the situation won't last forever. I just have to focus on breathing and relaxing.</td></tr>
</table>

Hierarchy List

Your fear:

Difficulty Ranking	Scene	Coping Statement(s)
1		
2		
3		
4		
5		
6		
7		
8		
9		
10		
11		
12		
13		
14		
15		
16		
17		
18		
19		
20		

Step 5: Begin Stress Inoculation

When you've completed the first four steps, you're ready to begin the stress-inoculation process. This involves relaxing, visualizing yourself in a stressful scene taken from your hierarchy, using your coping statements, and then monitoring your anxiety.

RELAX

Start the process by relaxing for ten to fifteen minutes. Use progressive muscle relaxation, cue-controlled relaxation, mindful breathing, safe-place visualization, or any combination that works for you. Then, when you're fully relaxed, review your list of coping statements for the scene you're going to visualize.

VISUALIZE THE SCENE

After you've relaxed, close your eyes and imagine yourself in the first (or next) scene from your hierarchy. Visualize as many details as you can: where you are, the time of day, who else is present, what makes it stressful, and any other details that help to bring the scene to life in your imagination. Also, do your best to imagine yourself in the scene as a calm, confident person capable of confronting the challenging situation. Take a few minutes to visualize as many of the details as you can in order to fully create the scene for yourself; try to make it as real as if you were really there.

BEGIN COPING

Once you've brought the scene to life in your imagination and you can picture yourself (and others) in the stressful scene, you can begin using your relaxation skills and coping statements to help you deal with your anxiety. Keep your eyes closed so that you can continue to imagine the scene. Then begin using one of the stress-reduction techniques that works most quickly for you, such as cue-controlled relaxation or mindful breathing. Also, begin repeating your coping statements for this scene, to help yourself relax even more.

Do your best to imagine this scene and yourself coping with it for thirty to sixty seconds, unless you start to feel overwhelmed by your anxiety (see "Monitor Your Anxiety," below).

MONITOR YOUR ANXIETY

Before beginning the stress-inoculation process, familiarize yourself with the following anxiety scale. This scale was created by psychologist Edmund Bourne to help people who are struggling with anxiety.[71] In essence, it describes how feelings of anxiety can escalate into a full-blown panic attack.

Throughout the stress-inoculation process you should monitor your anxiety level. Naturally, your anxiety will increase when you imagine yourself in a stressful situation or when you confront a stressful situation in real life. Very likely, your anxiety will increase from mild to moderate anxiety; that is, it will move from level 2 to level 3. However, if at any point you reach level 4, "marked anxiety," you should stop imagining yourself in the scene or withdraw from the scene in your real life. This is the point just before a panic attack develops, when you feel as though you are losing control. If during this exercise you reach level 4, marked anxiety, withdraw from the scene and begin using one of the relaxation skills to soothe yourself. You can use progressive muscle relaxation, cue-controlled relaxation, mindful breathing, safe-place visualization, or any combination of these that you choose.

Bourne Anxiety Scale		
Anxiety Level	**Category**	**Description**
7–10	Major panic attack	All of the same symptoms found in level 6; however, they are greatly exaggerated. In addition, there are feelings of terror, the fear of going crazy or dying, and the compulsion to escape.
6	Moderate panic attack	Heart palpitations, difficulty breathing, feeling disoriented or disconnected from reality, and panic due to the sense of loss of control.
5	Early panic	Heart pounding or beating irregularly, constricted breathing, spaciness or dizziness, fear of losing control, and the desire to escape.
4	Marked anxiety Caution: Stop Stress-Inoculation Process Here	Feeling uncomfortable or spacey, fast heartbeat, tight muscles, and doubts about your ability to maintain control.
3	Moderate anxiety	Feeling uncomfortable but still in control, heart starting to beat faster, more rapid breathing, and sweaty palms.
2	Mild anxiety	Nervous, muscle tension, and unsettled feeling (butterflies) in the stomach.

Reprinted with permission by New Harbinger Publications, Inc. *The Anxiety and Phobia Workbook*, Edmund Bourne (1995).

Provided that you don't reach level 4, the point of marked anxiety, continue to imagine yourself in your scene for thirty to sixty seconds. Then, when you're done, rate your anxiety using the Bourne scale. If your anxiety level is below level 2, meaning that you feel little to no anxiety, you're ready to move on to the next scene on your Hierarchy List. However, if your anxiety is still a level 2 or 3, use a few minutes of relaxation skills to soothe yourself and then repeat the process of imagining yourself coping in the scene until your anxiety level drops below level 2.

RELAX BETWEEN SCENES

Remember to use your relaxation skills (1) if you reach marked anxiety and (2) before moving on to a more difficult scene on your Hierarchy List. Use whatever skills provide you with the greatest sense of relaxation and calm.

PRACTICE REGULARLY

In order to ensure your success using stress inoculation, it's important that you use it regularly. Ideally, you should practice every day. In the beginning, you might practice for only fifteen minutes a day and then increase your sessions to thirty minutes a day once you've become more comfortable with the process. Be sure to stop if you get too tired.

Also, don't expect to conquer your entire hierarchy in just one or two sessions. During each session you may successfully cope with only two or three scenes on your list. That's enough. The next time you come back to the process, begin with the last scene you coped with, to ensure that the exposure process has been effective.

Step 6: Engage in Real-Life Exposure

After you've successfully coped with all of the items on your Hierarchy List using visualization and stress inoculation, the next step is to begin confronting the same feared situations in real life. Again, start by confronting the least fearful situations first, before working your way up your hierarchy to the most fearful situations. For many people, this is the most important and most powerful step in the entire treatment of personality disorders. This is so because successfully confronting your fears will improve your relationships, your abilities, and the way you think about yourself. Exposing yourself to feared situations takes courage and commitment, but without doing this step your rigid habits might not ever change.

When you begin confronting your feared situations in your real life, use the same relaxation skills and coping statements that you used in step 5. Obviously, some factors that you have not prepared for might arise, such as what another person might say, but just do your best to take on the challenge.

As in step 5, continue to monitor your anxiety level. Again, if your discomfort reaches marked anxiety, temporarily retreat from the situation, relax, reduce your anxiety, and then return to confront the situation as quickly as possible. Remember, your retreat should be only temporary, perhaps thirty minutes to an hour at most. Do your best not to give in to fear and run away, because in the future this will only reinforce your avoidance of the feared situation.

MAKE PREDICTIONS

When you begin confronting situations in real life, take a few minutes to write down your predictions of what you think will happen. Most people avoid feared situations because they think some sort of catastrophe will take place. However, this rarely happens. Record your prediction and rate how difficult you think the situation will be on a scale of 1 to 10. Then, after you confront the situation, see whether your predictions and ratings were accurate, and if they were not, ask yourself what that means about you and your abilities.

AVOID USING SAFETY BEHAVIORS

You probably know someone who carries a good-luck charm, goes to social events only if his or her best friend goes too, or engages in some type of unique behavior like tapping on the table eight times before doing something difficult. These are all forms of safety behaviors. *Safety behaviors* allow you to do something as long as they are performed before or after the difficult task. Most likely, no one knows about your safety behaviors other than yourself, so be honest with yourself. Do your best to eliminate all safety behaviors when performing stress inoculation or any other form of exposure. Remember, the purpose of these exercises is to recognize your own true power, not the power of your safety behaviors.

REWARD YOUR SUCCESSES

Rewards are much more powerful incentives than punishments, so give yourself a gift for each step you make toward achieving your goal. Find some healthy ways to reward your work, such as treating yourself to a nice meal after you practice stress inoculation or buying a new outfit after you complete your whole Hierarchy List. The more you reward yourself, the more motivated you'll be to continue with the entire process.

COPING WITH DIFFICULTIES DURING STRESS INOCULATION

If you experience any difficulties during the stress-inoculation process, such as your anxiety level remaining the same, try using one or more of the following suggestions.

Relax More Fully

If you can't relax before you begin or you find it difficult to relax in between scenes, take more time to relax or try using a different technique. For example, use the safe-place visualization to imagine yourself somewhere calm, safe, and peaceful. Or find a calming photograph and imagine yourself relaxing inside that image. Or record the instructions for one of the stress-reduction techniques and listen to it, to help you relax more fully.

Visualize More Fully

If your difficulty involves not being able to visualize the scene or if it seems flat, ineffective, or too unreal, spend some extra time engaging your imaginary senses. Allow yourself to imagine all of the sights in the scene: where you are, who you're with, the color of the room, the time of day, and so on. Then imagine the sounds you might hear; for example, music, the other person's voice, your own voice, the sounds of nearby animals, the blowing breezes, and so on. Then imagine any tactile sensations, such as the warmth of the sun on your skin, the feeling of your clothes on your body, the feeling of the ground beneath your feet, and so forth. Then imagine any scents or tastes in your scene: the smell of perfume or cologne, the taste of something you might be eating in the scene, the scent of flowers in the room or outside of the window, and so on.

Or, if you can, go to the real place where the scene will take place and take in all of the details. If it might be helpful, write them down and refer to these written details the next time you try to visualize the scene.

Recreate Your Hierarchy

It's fairly common for people to create hierarchies that have gaps in them, meaning step 4 (for example) is much more difficult than step 3. If this is true for your hierarchy, create an easier, transitional scene in between them. Conversely, if you don't experience any anxiety when visualizing your scenes, you probably need to make them more difficult. Remember, the point of the hierarchy is to help you succeed in meeting your challenges, not to stump you with a hierarchy that is too difficult or minimize your progress with steps that are too easy. Don't be afraid to rearrange your hierarchy or to add in-between steps if you find that to be necessary.

Change Your Coping Statements

As you engage in the stress-inoculation process, be aware that if your coping thoughts are not helping you, it's okay to change them at any time. If you need help, review the suggestions for creating effective coping statements in chapter 10 and in this chapter.

Setbacks Are Normal

Stress inoculation—and exposure of any kind—is difficult. Take your time when confronting the items on your hierarchy, and don't feel that you have to race to the finish. Find your own comfortable pace for completing each challenge on your hierarchy, and don't become upset or even surprised when a setback occurs. At some point in the stress-inoculation process, it's likely that you will experience some problem, like marked anxiety, fatigue, or the inability to move forward on your hierarchy. All of these experiences are normal, and they don't mean you've been defeated. Most setbacks are temporary ones, just as long as you decide to continue with the process.

OLIVIA'S EXAMPLE OF USING STRESS INOCULATION

Here's an example of using stress inoculation. Because Olivia struggled with obsessive-compulsive personality disorder, she was very afraid of making mistakes. At work, she was afraid of making mistakes on her reports; plus she was afraid that the other members of her production team would make mistakes. As a result, she worked very long hours checking and rechecking her work, which interfered with the time she could spend with her husband and children. At home, she was also afraid of making mistakes, such as taking the garbage out on the incorrect day for pickup and allowing her children to make errors on their homework. But most of all, she was afraid of making mistakes in public, such as embarrassing herself in a restaurant. All of these fears greatly interfered with her job performance and her family relationships, so one day she decided to try stress inoculation.

Olivia had already been practicing stress-reduction and relaxation techniques, so she was ready to begin the process. First she identified her fear as "I'm afraid of mistakes being made at work, at home, and in public, by me and by others." Then she built her Hierarchy List of sixteen fearful events that varied in difficulty from easy to hard. These events challenged her fear in different ways. For example, her events included "Allow kids to do homework by themselves," "Turn in team's report after I spend only thirty minutes reviewing it," and "Let Carl [her husband] take out the garbage, whether or not he forgets." Olivia then developed two specific coping statements to help her manage each stressful situation. For example, in response to one of the situations on her hierarchy that allowed her children or husband to do the dishes, Olivia wrote these coping statements: "Even if they're not 100 percent clean, it's very unlikely that anything will happen because of it" and "I'll just do my best to breathe and relax."

Then she began the stress-inoculation phase of relaxing, imagining herself in a scene from her Hierarchy List and visualizing herself coping by using her stress-reduction skills and coping thoughts. During each scene, she monitored her anxiety. A few times, her anxiety level rose to level 4, marked anxiety, so she had to stop and relax before continuing with the process of stress inoculation. However, she always returned to coping with each scene. When her anxiety level finally dropped below a level 2 for each situation, she practiced a few minutes of stress-reduction skills to help her relax, and then she moved on to imagining the next scene on her hierarchy. It took Olivia nineteen days to successfully imagine herself coping with all sixteen situations on her Hierarchy List.

Then Olivia began confronting each situation in real life, beginning with the easiest scene of her hierarchy. Again, there were times when her anxiety got too high and she had to temporarily withdraw from the situation, but she always went back and continued coping. Olivia worked at her own pace and used rewards to motivate her progress (such as buying a new CD and fresh flowers for her desk), and after two months of work, she was able to complete all the items on her hierarchy.

REVIEW STRESS-INOCULATION OUTLINE

As you can see, there are many steps in the stress-inoculation treatment. In order to feel comfortable using stress inoculation, you might need to review this section of the chapter several times. Do not feel rushed to begin. Make sure you understand the treatment before using it. In order to remind yourself about the steps of the treatment, use the following Stress-Inoculation Outline:

Stress-Inoculation Outline

1. Practice relaxation skills.

    a. Progressive muscle relaxation

    b. Cue-controlled relaxation

    c. Mindful breathing

    d. Safe-place visualization

2. Choose a fear to confront.

    a. Use negative core belief or "I'm afraid of…," if necessary.

    b. State your fear as something specific that can be challenged in a series of steps.

3. Build an exposure hierarchy.

    a. Record ten to twenty situations on your Hierarchy List that challenge your fear and that range in difficulty from easy to hard.

    b. Use four variables to create different levels of difficulty.

        i. How close you are to your feared experience

        ii. How much time you spend in contact with your feared experience

        iii. How fearful each step is

        iv. How much support you receive during the feared event

    c. Make sure the steps increase in difficulty in a consistent way.

    d. Plan situations that you can set up easily in the near future.

    e. Prepare for real-life situations.

4. Develop your coping statements.

    a. Create one or two coping statements for each situation and record them on your Hierarchy List.

    b. Address both thoughts and feelings related to anxiety.

5. Begin stress inoculation.

    a. Relax for ten to fifteen minutes before starting.

    b. Visualize as many of the details of the scene as possible.

    c. Begin coping, using your relaxation skills and coping statements.

    d. Imagine yourself coping in the scene for thirty to sixty seconds.

e. Monitor your anxiety and stop if you reach level 4, "marked anxiety," on the Bourne scale.

f. When you've completed the scene, rate your anxiety.

   i. Repeat the scene if your anxiety is still a level 2 or 3.

   ii. Move on to the next scene if your anxiety is below level 2.

g. Relax between the scenes and if you reach marked anxiety.

h. Practice regularly and don't expect to conquer your entire hierarchy in just one or two sessions.

6. Engage in real-life exposure.

a. Use the same relaxation skills and coping statements used in step 5.

b. Make predictions of how difficult a situation will be using a scale of 1 to 10.

c. Start by confronting the least fearful scenes on your Hierarchy List before moving up.

d. Continue to monitor your anxiety level; if your discomfort reaches level 4, temporarily retreat from the situation and then return to confront the situation as quickly as possible.

e. Avoid using safety behaviors.

f. After confronting a situation, determine whether your prediction was accurate.

g. Reward your successes.

EMOTION EXPOSURE

Now it's time to learn another form of exposure treatment. *Emotion exposure* is a skill that will help you learn to tolerate your feelings and to not fear them. As with other forms of exposure, emotion exposure will help you stay in contact with your emotions—even the very strong ones—instead of avoiding or resisting them. As you stay in contact with them, you'll recognize that your emotions shift and change over time, and that they very naturally diminish in intensity.

This technique builds on the emotion awareness skills that you learned earlier in this book. You should have already practiced emotional journaling and being mindful of your emotions without judgment (in chapter 7) before trying this exercise. Before using emotion exposure, review your Emotional Journals. (Hopefully, you've completed more than one.) First notice if there are any emotions that came up frequently, especially distressing ones like anger, loneliness, or fear. Then notice if there were any emotions that you ignored, resisted, or avoided. Usually, when you use one of these strategies instead of dealing with the emotion, you make the situation worse. For example, if you felt embarrassed in a social situation and then lashed out at another person instead of coping with the emotion you were feeling, you probably damaged that relationship. Emotions that show up repeatedly or are handled in ineffective ways are good targets for emotion exposure. These are the emotions that you need help with, to learn how to confront and tolerate them.

Learning how to stay in contact with your emotions and cope with them is an extremely important skill for anyone struggling with a personality disorder, but it's especially important for people who are frequently overwhelmed by their emotions, such as those struggling with antisocial, borderline, histrionic, and narcissistic personality disorders. In addition, this skill is very important for people who react in destructive ways to their strong emotions, such as those who self-mutilate or who lash out angrily at others.

The technique described here is based on the emotion exposure exercise in *The Dialectical Behavior Therapy Skills Workbook*.[63]

Britney's Example of Using Emotion Exposure

Britney struggled with borderline personality disorder. She frequently felt lonely, angry, and frightened, especially about the possibility of being abandoned by her friends. One night, her friend Lindsay cancelled their plans at the very last minute and Britney felt overwhelmed with anger and loneliness. In response, she first raged at Lindsay and then engaged in self-harm by cutting herself. A few days later, Britney recognized that she had once again been overwhelmed by her painful emotions, and she promised herself to try something different. She wasn't sure if emotion exposure would help her, but she decided to give it a good try.

She began by choosing a time and place where she wouldn't be disturbed for ten minutes. Then she sat on a comfortable chair and began to breathe, feeling the air rise and fall in her lungs, and noticing the tension in her neck.). Then she brought to mind the troubling emotions she'd experienced when Lindsay cancelled on her and began to imagine herself back in that situation. At first, it just felt like anger, a sharp, painful anger that was extremely intense. But after a few minutes, she also recognized that she was feeling afraid of being abandoned. She tried to describe this other feeling but could only manage to come up with two words: "big" and "alone." As she continued to observe the emotion she was feeling, fairly quickly she felt the urge to stop the breathing exercise and to call her friend to yell at her. But she resisted the urge and didn't do that.

Instead, Britney observed what it felt like to not act on her emotions. It was very uncomfortable, but she did it anyway. Then she noticed that she was thinking judgments about herself and her friend: judgments that stated she was "incapable of having a real friendship" and that "Lindsay was a crappy friend." These judgments made Britney feel sad, but she did her best to just observe the judgments and then to let them go. She also did her best to stay focused on how she was feeling. A few minutes later, she recognized that her original anger had diminished in intensity, and that now she was feeling sad instead of abandoned. After five minutes, she finished the exercise by doing some mindful breathing, and when it was over, she was happily surprised to find that she had been able to tolerate her emotions for that long without expressing anger at herself or at Lindsay. Britney promised herself that she would continue practicing paying attention to her emotions.

EXERCISE: Emotion Exposure

Before beginning this exercise, pick a troubling emotional experience from your journal and imagine yourself back in that situation. Visualize what happened and try to see as many of the details as possible. Then when you start to feel that emotion again, begin the exercise. If at any point your anxiety reaches level 4 on the Bourne Anxiety Scale (see the instructions for stress inoculation above), take a short break, relax for a while, and then return to the exercise.

You can either read the instructions as you proceed or you can record them and listen to them while you are practicing.

To begin, take a few slow breaths in and out. Feel the breath entering your body and expanding your lungs and abdominal muscles. As you do this, notice how your body feels, especially your face, neck, shoulders, and abdomen. (Pause here to notice your breathing and body.)

Now notice the emotion you're feeling. Name it if you can and describe it to yourself. Notice whether it's weak or strong. Is it sharp or dull? Is it growing, stable, or diminishing? If it helps, identify any sounds, colors, or other unique qualities associated with your emotion. Take a minute to describe all the qualities of your emotion, and do your best to stay connected to it. If you get distracted, simply return your focus to your emotion. (Pause here to describe your emotion.)

Now notice any changes in the way you're feeling. Is your emotion becoming more or less intense? Find a few words to describe any changes you recognize. Also notice if there are any additional emotions that you're now experiencing, no matter how small they might be. Try to name them and describe their qualities, too. (Pause here to describe any changes in your emotion plus any other feelings you're experiencing.)

As you continue to focus on your emotions, you might recognize the desire to stop this exercise, distract yourself, block your feelings, or push away them away. That's normal, but do your best to resist those desires. Return your focus to your emotions for just a few minutes longer and continue to observe what they are and how they change. (Pause here to recognize any desires to block your emotions.)

If you do notice a desire to act on your emotions, recognize what it feels like not to act. Observe how it feels not to avoid your emotions, block them, or lash out because of them. Be aware of experiencing feeling your emotions without acting on your impulses. Observe what it's like to sit quietly with your emotions without doing anything about them. Remind yourself that emotions come and go like ocean waves that rise and fall. As soon as one passes, there may be another behind it, but there are also periods of calm. Similarly, if you're currently experiencing a distressing emotion that creates the desire for action, recognize that it too will pass, and know that soon you'll experience a period of calm. Try to notice any periods of calm. Continue to watch the wave of emotion as it passes. (Pause here to recognize the experience of not acting on your emotions.)

Now notice any judgments that arise about yourself, others, your emotion, this exercise, or anything else. Do your best to let go of those judgments without getting connected to them. (Pause here to recognize and let go of any judgments.)

Continue to observe your emotions. Notice any changes, no matter how small they might be. Recognize any differences in intensity, no matter how minor. Note any additional emotions that you've started to feel and do your best to stay connected to them without resisting or avoiding them. (Pause here to notice any changes in your emotions.)

When you're ready, finish this exercise with a few minutes of mindful breathing, watching your breath rise and fall. Then return your focus to the room and observe any changes in the way you feel. Note the effect this exercise had on you, no matter how small.

When you begin practicing emotion exposure, plan to spend just five minutes doing this exercise. Then, as you become more comfortable focusing on your emotions and tolerating them, you can spend longer periods of time, like ten to fifteen minutes. As you grow more comfortable tolerating your emotions, you'll find that this exercise becomes easier. And always remember to end the exercise with mindful breathing or another stress-reduction technique to relax.

IN CONCLUSION

Exposure is a very powerful treatment that is used for many mental health issues. It does take a lot of courage to face the things you are most afraid of, but the payoff is often very rewarding. Remember to practice at your own pace when using exposure of any kind, and don't allow yourself to be discouraged by any setbacks. They're sure to happen, but they don't have to mean defeat if you're willing to go back to the process and try again.

PART III

Post-Treatment Care

CHAPTER 12

Maintain Your Progress and Prevent Setbacks

Hopefully, you've had many successes with learning and using the various skills in this book. Maybe you've filled your life with activities that lead to mastery and give you pleasure, challenged your negative automatic thoughts successfully, created healthier core beliefs, learned how to relax, identified your emotions, solved some old problems, learned how to communicate more effectively, and used exposure effectively to tackle challenges and face your fears and emotions. You've probably been working very hard for many weeks or even months to change the habits of your personality disorder. Now it's important for you to maintain and protect the progress you've made. For that reason, the last step of this cognitive behavioral therapy treatment for personality disorders is to develop two plans, one to help you preserve the progress you've made and the other to prevent setbacks.

CREATE A MAINTENANCE PLAN

In order to maintain the progress you've made using this workbook, you should consider choosing a handful of skills that you're willing to practice every day. This doesn't have to be a very time-consuming process. Each day, your entire maintenance plan should take only about fifteen to thirty minutes from start to finish. Most importantly, it should help you focus on your thoughts, feelings, and actions. Consider doing your maintenance plan shortly after you wake up and think of it as a healthy way to start your day. Or you can do it before you go to bed and think of it as a good way to clear your head before you go to sleep. Whatever time you choose, do it at the same time every day to establish it as a healthy habit.

Ideally, your maintenance plan should include the following:

- Mindful breathing (five to ten minutes)

- Cue-controlled relaxation or safe-place visualization (five to ten minutes)

- Being mindful of your emotions without judgment (three to five minutes)

- Activity scheduling for that day (or the following day), including one pleasurable and one mastery activity (two minutes)

In addition, continue to use your other coping skills as needed, such as writing in your Challenge Your Unhelpful Thinking Styles worksheet, practicing problem-solving skills, engaging in coping imagery, and so on.

PREPARE FOR SETBACKS

In addition to maintaining your progress, you also need to be prepared for setbacks. Progress toward any goal never goes in a straight line in only one direction. Usually, it's more like a roller coaster, with ups and downs and twists and turns. As you continue using the various skills in this workbook, you'll experience healthy changes in the way you think about yourself, you'll feel better, you'll recognize improvements in your relationships, and you'll take on challenges that you previously avoided. Overall, you'll gain confidence in your ability to enrich and improve your life.

However, you will also experience some unexpected twists and turns, as well as some setbacks. These cannot be avoided. Some days your new coping skills will be easy to use, and other days they'll seem impossible. Hopefully, such setbacks won't erase all of the gains you've made and your difficult days won't stand in the way of your progress or meeting your goals.

Most setbacks occur because the person isn't sufficiently prepared to take on a high-risk situation. Unfortunately, many people attribute their setbacks to their own personal shortcomings and say to themselves or to others, "See? I can't change; I'll always be defective. I may as well give up." But this simply isn't true. The key to success is to learn from your mistakes and prepare for the future. Instead of criticizing yourself, the next time you experience a setback in your treatment, try saying, "I just wasn't ready for this situation; I'll work even harder to practice my skills, and I'll be ready the next time."

USE A RELAPSE PREVENTION PROGRAM

To help you cope with your setbacks you'll need a plan, such as the relapse prevention program developed by psychologists G. Alan Marlatt and Judith Gordon.[72] This program was developed for people who are struggling with substance addictions, but the recommendations are good advice for anyone, no matter what kind of habit you're dealing with and trying to change. For your purposes, you can think of a relapse as any setback that interferes with your treatment.

Identify Your High-Risk Situations

The first step is to be prepared for high-risk situations. During such situations you're more likely to feel vulnerable and to experience a setback in your progress. So you should be prepared to use your coping skills. Perhaps you already know what some of your high-risk situations are. If so, write them down. If not, Marlatt and Gordon have identified three common high-risk situations. They are as follows:

1. When you're already feeling sad, anxious, angry, frustrated, or bored.[72]

2. When you're experiencing a problem with another person, such as a conflict with a loved one.[73]

3. When you're feeling peer pressure in a social situation.[73]

During such situations you're likely to forget about using your coping skills. Or if you do remember, you might feel too tired, scared, or unmotivated to use them. Therefore, do your best to prepare for these situations and others like them.

Right now, take a few minutes to identify your own high-risk situations. These are situations in which you'll experience an exceptional amount of stress. Write them down. Then ask yourself whether these are situations you can avoid or if they're situations you must confront. If you do have to confront them, make a relapse road map, as shown below, to prepare yourself.

Three high-risk situations I expect to confront in the near future are:

1. _____

2. _____

3. _____

Make a Relapse Road Map

If you must face a high-risk situation, Marlatt and Gordon recommend making a relapse road map to help you deal with it.[72] First you identify the different ways you can cope with the high-risk situation. Then you identify the possible outcomes of using each of those coping methods. And finally, based on the possible outcomes, you select the best method to cope with the situation.

For example, Vivian, who struggles with personality disorder not otherwise specified, was planning to attend a social event where she knew she would feel very anxious; this was a high-risk situation for her. So she decided to make a relapse road map. She understood that it would be helpful to use a stress-reduction skill that would help her to relax at the event. On her relapse road map she included progressive muscle relaxation, mindful breathing, and the body scan. Then she considered the possible outcomes of using each skill. She decided that although progressive muscle relaxation would be helpful, it wasn't something she could use in front of everyone. The body scan would also be helpful, but it took too long to use, and usually she felt so relaxed after doing it that she fell asleep. So she decided to use mindful breathing, which was both fast and effective.

For each of the high-risk situations that you expect to confront in the near future, list at least three possible coping skills you can use and their possible outcomes. Then choose the skill that is most likely to help you.

1. High-risk situation 1: _____

   A. Coping strategy: _____

   A. Possible outcome: _____

  B. Coping strategy: _____

  B. Possible outcome: _____

  C. Coping strategy: _____

  C. Possible outcome: _____

2. High-risk situation 2: _____

  A. Coping strategy: _____

  A. Possible outcome: _____

  B. Coping strategy: _____

  B. Possible outcome: _____

  C. Coping strategy: _____

  C. Possible outcome: _____

3. High-risk situation 3: _____

  A. Coping strategy: _____

  A. Possible outcome: _____

  B. Coping strategy: _____

  B. Possible outcome: _____

  C. Coping strategy: _____

  C. Possible outcome: _____

Reduce the Stress in Your Life

When you're feeling stressed-out and overwhelmed by the demands of life, you're also more likely to revert back to your old habits. Therefore, do your best to recognize and understand how stress affects you and find a skill to reduce it as best you can.

For example, maybe you experience stress as racing thoughts. If so, try using your Challenge Your Unhelpful Thinking Styles worksheet to challenge those thoughts. Or perhaps you recognize stress as muscle tension in your body. If so, try using progressive muscle relaxation or a similar technique to relieve your muscle tension. Or maybe you experience stress as an emotion. In this case, you can try emotion exposure or a stress-reduction technique, such as mindful breathing, to soothe yourself. Finally, you might experience stress as weariness or sluggishness. If so, try scheduling some pleasurable activities into your life and see whether that relieves the strain of being stressed-out.

Act Healthy

To make your daily life feel more fulfilling, Marlatt and Gordon recommend adding healthy activities to it.[72] Many people with personality disorders don't participate in recreational activities and neglect having fun. If you're one of these, review chapter 4, especially the Big List of Pleasurable Activities, and do your best to schedule at least one pleasurable activity every day. And if there's not enough time in your day, see if there are any unpleasurable or unhealthy activities that you can eliminate, such as obsessively reviewing your work, to make time and space for something that will add fun and pleasure to your life.

Set Reasonable and Measurable Goals

A goal is something that you work hard to achieve. The purpose of this workbook is to help you achieve the goal of changing your long-standing habits. But each person will have a different goal (or goals) since each person has different habits to change. For that reason, devote some time to setting your own goals and make sure that they are both reasonable and measurable, which means that you can achieve them with a realistic amount of effort and that you can keep track of them.

For example, the following goal is reasonable but unmeasurable because it's not specific: "I want to do better at work." "Better at work" could mean anything from "make better coffee for my boss" to "write better reports." To make it measurable, you'd need to identify something specific that you can keep track of, something that you can measure. In comparison, the following goals are both reasonable and measurable:

- "Every day at work I want to use at least one new coping skill."

- "Every week I want to schedule at least one pleasurable activity."

- "Every weekend I want to use my assertive communication skills at least once."

- "Two afternoons a month I will spend time developing new core beliefs."

Of course, your goals can be whatever you want them to be. And feel free to move at your own pace. Remember, your old habits won't change overnight; doing so will require months of practice, and that's okay. Pick goals that are important and that will help you to change the habits of your personality disorder. Just make sure that your goals are reasonable and measurable so that you can keep track of your progress.

Then, after a few weeks of working toward your goals, ask yourself if you're achieving them. If the answer is yes, great! You're on your way to becoming a healthier, happier person. But if the answer is no, ask yourself, why? Maybe the goals you picked are too hard, too unreasonable, or not specific enough. For example, some people say their goal is to "act normally," but this is not specific. First of all, who decides what is normal? And second, there's no way to measure it. Be fair to yourself. In the beginning, pick smaller goals that you can achieve easily, and then as your treatment progresses and you gain more skill and confidence, you can try tackling your bigger goals.

Now, record three small, reasonable, measurable goals. Note one for yourself, one for your career, and one for your relationships. Then review them in eight to twelve weeks to determine whether you're getting closer to achieving them.

1. My goal for myself is: _____

2. My goal for my career is: _____

3. My goal for my relationships is: _____

Keep Track of Your Successes

The next step in the relapse prevention program is to build your *self-efficacy*, which means your own sense of effectiveness and self-worth. One way to do this is to keep track of your successes, no matter how small they are. Think back to when you first started using the skills in this workbook and then record all of the following:

- Pleasurable and mastery activities you've tried

- Thought Journals you've completed

- Unhelpful thinking styles you've challenged

- Negative core beliefs that you've identified and tested

- Positive core beliefs that you've developed

- Stress-reduction, relaxation, and mindfulness skills that you've used

- Judgments that you've identified

- Emotions that you've identified and described

- Problems that you've solved

- Assertive communication skills that you've tried

- Coping imagery that you've used

- Stress inoculations that you've tried

- Any other successes that you've experienced

Continue keeping track of all your successes from now on. You can keep track of them anywhere you like, such as on a piece of paper or in a file in your computer, but for a special sense of accomplishment consider buying a small notebook that you devote exclusively to your successes. Hopefully, recording these successes will build and strengthen your belief that you are capable of coping with difficult situations in new, healthy ways.

Make a Relapse Plan

Despite your best efforts to use your coping skills and to follow the relapse prevention program, there will still be times when you'll return to using your old habits, you'll think about the world in your old ways, and you'll feel lousy. This is normal and it doesn't mean that you're a failure. It just means that some days will be tougher than others.

In order to be prepared for such days, you should develop a relapse plan that includes social support and helpful skills. First make a list of anyone you can call when you're feeling distressed, anxious, or overwhelmed. That person could be a friend, family member, 12-step sponsor, therapist, someone from work, your minister, imam, priest, or rabbi, a crisis-hotline volunteer, or anyone else who is usually available. Keep that person's phone number with you in your wallet so that you can call him or her the next time you need support. Sometimes just hearing a familiar voice will be enough to lift your spirits.

Next, find a few skills or activities that regularly improve your mood, such as mindful breathing or taking a walk in the park. Keep a list of those activities with you too, so the next time you're feeling overwhelmed and can't remember what to do, you can look at your list and remind yourself.

And, lastly, if you're still feeling exceptionally defeated or distressed and nothing seems to be helping you, please consult a mental health care professional for advice, someone such as a psychologist, psychiatrist, social worker, counselor, or therapist.

IN CONCLUSION

The key to improving your life and preventing setbacks from overwhelming you is to continue using the coping skills that you learned how to use in this workbook. Practice them as frequently as possible—ideally, every day—until they become a regular part of how you think, act, and cope with your feelings. However, even when they have become a part of your daily life, you should still be prepared for high-risk situations that might lead to setbacks.

I wish you great success as you continue to use this workbook to improve your life. Remember, you don't have to do it all perfectly, nor do the changes you want to experience have to come very quickly. Find the skills and the pace that are best for you and continue to work hard, despite occasional setbacks. I know that you will find success. Good luck.

References

1. American Psychiatric Association. 2000. *Diagnostic and Statistical Manual of Mental Disorders.* 4th ed. text revision. Washington, DC: American Psychiatric Association.

2. Grant, B. F., D. S. Hasin, F. S. Stinson, D. A. Dawson, W. J. Ruan, R. B. Goldstein, S. M. Smith, T. D. Saha, and B. Huang. 2004. Prevalence, correlates, and disability of personality disorders in the United States: Results from the National Epidemiologic Survey on alcohol and related conditions. *Journal of Clinical Psychiatry* 65(7):948-958.

3. Ekselius, L., M. Tillfors, T. Furmark, and M. Fredrikson. 2001. Personality disorders in the general population: *DSM-IV* and *ICD-10* defined prevalence as related to sociodemographic profile. *Personality and Individual Differences* 30(2):311-320.

4. Moran, P. 1999. The epidemiology of antisocial personality disorder. *Social Psychiatry and Psychiatric Epidemiology* 34(5):231-242.

5. Robertson, R. G., R. G. Bankier, and L. Schwartz. 1987. The female offender: A Canadian study. *Canadian Journal of Psychiatry* 32(9):749-755.

6. Martin, R. L., C. R. Cloninger, S. B. Guze, and P. J. Clayton. 1985. Mortality in a follow-up of 500 psychiatric outpatients: II. Cause-specific mortality. *Archives of General Psychiatry* 42(1):58-66.

7. Black, D. W., C. H. Baumgard, and C. E. Bell. 1995. A 16- to 45-year follow-up of 71 men with antisocial personality disorder. *Comprehensive Psychiatry* 36(2):130-140.

8. McDonald, A. S., and G. C. L. Davey. 1996. Psychiatric disorders and accidental injury. *Clinical Psychology Review* 16(2):105-127.

9. Rydelius, P. A. 1988. The development of antisocial behaviour and sudden violent death. *Acta Psychiatrica Scandinavica* 77(4):398-403.

10. Grant, B. F., D. S. Hasin, F. S. Stinson, D. A. Dawson, S. P. Chou, W. J. Ruan, and B. Huang. 2005. Co-occurrence of 12-month mood and anxiety disorders and personality disorders in the US: Results from the national epidemiologic survey on alcohol and related conditions. *Journal of Psychiatric Research* 39(1):1-9.

11. Grant, B. F., F. S. Stinson, D. A. Dawson, S. P. Chou, W. J. Ruan, and R. P. Pickering. 2004. Co-occurrence of 12-month alcohol and drug use disorders and personality disorders in the United States: Results from the national epidemiologic survey on alcohol and related conditions. *Archives of General Psychiatry* 61(4):361-368.

12. Slutske, W. S., S. Eisen, H. Xian, W. R. True, M. J. Lyons, J. Goldberg, and M. Tsuang. 2001. A twin study of the association between pathological gambling and antisocial personality disorder. *Journal of Abnormal Psychology* 110(2):297-308.

13. Koenigsberg, H. W., P. D. Harvey, V. Mitropoulou, A. S. New, M. Goodman, J. Silverman, M. Serby, F. Schopick, and L. J. Siever. 2001. Are the interpersonal and identity disturbances in the borderline personality disorder criteria linked to the traits of affective instability and impulsivity? *Journal of Personality Disorders* 15(4):358-370.

14. Linehan, M. M. 1993. *Cognitive-Behavioral Treatment of Borderline Personality Disorder.* New York: The Guilford Press.

15. Black, D. W., N. Blum, B. Pfohl, and N. Hale. 2004. Suicidal behavior in borderline personality disorder: Prevalence, risk factors, prediction, and prevention. *Journal of Personality Disorders* 18(3):226-239.

16. Paris, J., and H. Zweig-Frank. 2001. The 27-year follow-up of patients with borderline personality disorder. *Comprehensive Psychiatry* 42(6):482-487.

17. Zanarini, M. C., F. R. Frankenburg, E. D. Dubo, A. E. Sickel, A. Trikha, A. Levin, and V. Reynolds. 1998. Axis I comorbidity of borderline personality disorder. *American Journal of Psychiatry* 155(12):1733-1739.

18. Johnson, D. M., M. T. Shea, S. Yen, C. L. Battle, C. Zlotnick, C. A. Sanislow, C. M. Grilo, A. E. Skodol, D. S. Bender, T. H. McGlashan, et al. 2003. Gender differences in borderline personality disorder: Findings from the Collaborative Longitudinal Personality Disorders Study. *Comprehensive Psychiatry* 44(4):284-292.

19. Frankenburg, F. R., and M. C. Zanarini. 2004. The association between borderline personality disorder and chronic medical illnesses, poor health-related lifestyle choices, and costly forms of health care utilization. *Journal of Clinical Psychiatry* 65(12):1660-1665.

20. Widiger, T. A., and M. M. Weissman. 1991. Epidemiology of borderline personality disorder. *Hospital and Community Psychiatry* 42(10):1015-1021.

21. Becker, D., and S. Lamb. 1994. Sex bias in the diagnosis of borderline personality disorder and post-traumatic stress disorder. *Professional Psychology: Research and Practice* 25(1):55-61.

22. Overholser, J. C. 1996. The dependent personality and interpersonal problems. *Journal of Nervous and Mental Disease* 184(1):8-16.

23. Chioqueta, A. P., and T. C. Stiles. 2004. Assessing suicide risk in Cluster C personality disorders. *Crisis* 25(3):128-133.

24. Torgersen, S., E. Kringlen, and V. Cramer. 2001. The prevalence of personality disorders in a community sample. *Archives of General Psychiatry* 58(6):590-596.

25. Wink, P. 1991. Two faces of narcissism. *Journal of Personality and Social Psychology* 61(4):590-597.

26. Bushman, B. J., and R. F. Baumeister. 1998. Threatened egotism, narcissism, self-esteem, and direct and displaced aggression: Does self-love or self-hate lead to violence? *Journal of Personality and Social Psychology* 75(1):219-229.

27. Campbell, W. K., and C. A. Foster. 2002. Narcissism and commitment in romantic relationships: An investment model analysis. *Personality and Social Psychology Bulletin* 28(4):484-495.

28. Schiavone, P., S. Dorz, D. Conforti, C. Scarso, and G. Borgherini. 2004. Comorbidity of *DSM-IV* personality disorders in unipolar and bipolar affective disorders: A comparative study. *Psychological Reports* 95(1):121-128.

29. Oldham, J. M., A. E. Skodol, H. D. Kellman, S. E. Hyler, N. Doidge, L. Rosnick, and P. E. Gallaher. 1995. Comorbidity of axis I and axis II disorders. *American Journal of Psychiatry* 152(4):571-578.

30. Casillas, A., and L. A. Clark. 2002. Dependency, impulsivity, and self-harm: Traits hypothesized to underlie the association between Cluster B personality and substance use disorders. *Journal of Personality Disorders* 16(5):424-436.

31. Blaszczynski, A., and Z. Steel. 1998. Personality disorders among pathological gamblers. *Journal of Gambling Studies* 14(1):51-71.

32. Brunton, J. N., J. H. Lacey, and G. Waller. 2005. Narcissism and eating characteristics in young nonclinical women. *Journal of Nervous and Mental Disease* 193(2):140-143.

33. Links, P. S., B. Gould, and R. Ratnayake. 2003. Assessing suicidal youth with antisocial, borderline, or narcissistic personality disorder. *Canadian Journal of Psychiatry* 48(5):301-310.

34. Perry, J. C. 1989. Personality disorders, suicide, and self-destructive behavior. In *Suicide: Understanding and Responding: Harvard Medical School Perspectives,* edited by D. Jacobs and H. N. Brown, 157-169. Madison, CT: International Universities Press, Inc.

35. Golomb, M., M. Fava, M. Abraham, and J. F. Rosenbaum. 1995. Gender differences in personality disorders. *American Journal of Psychiatry* 152(4):579-582.

36. Beck, A. T., A. Freeman, and J. Pretzer. 1990. *Cognitive Therapy of Personality Disorders*. New York: The Guilford Press.

37. Rasmussen, P. R. 2005. The schizoid prototype. In *Personality-Guided Cognitive-Behavioral Therapy*, 73-87. Washington, DC: American Psychological Association.

38. Birtchnell, J. 1996. Detachment. In *Personality Characteristics of the Personality Disordered*, edited by C. G. Costello, 173-205. New York: Wiley.

39. Rodriguez Solano, J. J., and M. Gonzalez De Chavez. 2000. Premorbid personality disorders in schizophrenia. *Schizophrenia Research* 44(20):137-144.

40. Rouff, L. 2000. Schizoid personality traits among the homeless mentally ill: A quantitative and qualitative report. *Journal of Social Distress and the Homeless* 9(2):127-141.

41. Livesley, W. J., K. L. Jang, and P. A. Vernon. 1998. Phenotypic and genetic structure of traits delineating personality disorder. *Archives of General Psychiatry* 55(10):941-948.

42. Donegan, N. H., C. A. Sanislow, H. P. Blumberg, R. K. Fulbright, C. Lacadie, P. Skudlarski, J. C. Gore, I. R. Olson, T. H. McGlashan, and B. E. Wexler. 2003. Amygdala hyperreactivity in borderline personality disorder: Implications for emotional dysregulation. *Biological Psychiatry* 54(11):1284-1293.

43. Kasen, S., P. Cohen, A. E. Skodol, J. G. Johnson, E. Smailes, and J. S. Brook. 1999. The influence of child and adolescent psychiatric disorders on young adult personality disorder. *American Journal of Psychiatry* 156:(10)1529-1535.

44. Kim-Cohen, J., T. E. Moffitt, A. Taylor, S. J. Pawlby, and A. Caspi. 2005. Maternal depression and children's antisocial behavior: Nature and nurture effects. *Archives of General Psychiatry* 62(2):173-181.

45. Caspi, A., T. E. Moffitt, J. Morgan, M. Rutter, A. Taylor, L. Arseneault, L. Tully, C. Jacobs, and J. Kim-Cohen. 2004. Maternal expressed emotion predicts children's antisocial behavior problems: Using monozygotic-twin differences to identify environmental effects on behavioral development. *Developmental Psychology* 40(2):149-161.

46. Caspi, A., T. E. Moffitt, D. L. Newman, and P. A. Silva. 1996. Behavioural observations at age 3 years predict adult psychiatric disorders. Longitudinal evidence from a birth cohort. *Archives of General Psychiatry* 53(11):1033-1039.

47. Bierer, L. M., R. Yehuda, J. Schmeidler, V. Mitropoulou, A. S. New, J. M. Silverman, and L. J. Siever. 2003. Abuse and neglect in childhood: Relationship to personality disorder diagnoses. *CNS Spectrums* 8(10):737-740, 749-754.

48. Chang, C. J., W. J. Chen, S. K. Liu, J. J. Chang, W. C. Ou-Yang, H. J. Chang, H. Y. Lane, S. K. Lin, T. W. Yang, and H. G. Hwu. 2002. Morbidity risk of psychiatric disorders among the first degree relatives of schizophrenia patients in Taiwan. *Schizophrenia Bulletin* 28(3):379-392.

49. Hoek, H. W., E. Susser, K. A. Buck, and L. H. Lumey. 1996. Schizoid personality disorder after prenatal exposure to famine. *American Journal of Psychiatry* 153(12):1637-1639.

50. Smith, C. A., and D. P. Farrington. 2004. Continuities in antisocial behavior and parenting across three generations. *Journal of Child Psychology and Psychiatry* 45(2):230-247.

51. Butler, A. C., J. E. Chapman, E. M. Forman, and A. T. Beck. 2006. The empirical status of cognitive-behavioral therapy: A review of meta-analyses. *Clinical Psychology Review* 26(1):17-31.

52. Bateman, A. W., and P. Fonagy. 2000. Effectiveness of psychotherapeutic treatment of personality disorder. *British Journal of Psychiatry* 177:138-143.

53. Leichsenring, F., and E. Leibing. 2003. The effectiveness of psychodynamic therapy and cognitive behavior therapy in the treatment of personality disorders: A meta-analysis. *American Journal of Psychiatry* 160(7):1223-1232.

54. Svartberg, M., T. C. Stiles, and M. H. Seltzer. 2004. Randomized, controlled trial of the effectiveness of short-term dynamic psychotherapy and cognitive therapy for Cluster C personality disorders. *American Journal of Psychiatry* 161(5):810-817.

55. Beck, J. S. 1998. Complex cognitive therapy treatment for personality disorder patients. *Bulletin of the Menninger Clinic* 62(2):170-194.

56. Bienenfeld, D. 2007. Cognitive therapy of patients with personality disorders. *Psychiatric Annals* 37(2):133-139.

57. McKay, M., M. Davis, and P. Fanning. 1997. *Thoughts & Feelings: Taking Control of Your Moods & Your Life*. Oakland, CA: New Harbinger Publications.

58. Beck, A. T., A. J. Rush, B. F. Shaw, and G. Emery. 1979. *Cognitive Therapy of Depression*. New York: The Guilford Press.

59. Greenberger, D., and C. Padesky. 1995. *Mind Over Mood*. New York: The Guilford Press.

60. Young, J. 1990. *Cognitive Therapy for Personality Disorders: A Schema-Focused Approach*. Sarasota, FL: Professional Resource Exchange.

61. McKay, M., and P. Fanning. 1991. *Prisoners of Belief: Exposing & Changing Beliefs That Control Your Life*. Oakland, CA: New Harbinger Publications.

62. Davis, M., M. McKay, and E. R. Eshelman. 2008. *The Relaxation and Stress Reduction Workbook*, 6th ed. Oakland, CA: New Harbinger Publications.

63. McKay, M., J. C. Wood, and J. Brantley. 2007. *The Dialectical Behavior Therapy Skills Workbook: Practical DBT Exercises for Learning Mindfulness, Interpersonal Effectiveness, Emotion Regulation & Distress Tolerance*. Oakland, CA: New Harbinger Publications.

64. Jacobson, E. 1938. *Progressive Relaxation*. Chicago: University of Chicago Press.

65. Babyak, M., J. A. Blumenthal, S. Herman, P. Khatri, M. Doraiswamy, K. Moore, W. E. Craighead, T. T. Baldwicz, and K. R. Krishnan. 2000. Exercise treatment for major depression: Maintenance of therapeutic benefit at 10 months. *Psychosomatic Medicine* 62(5):633-638.

66. D'Zurilla, T. J., and M. R. Goldfried. 1971. Problem solving and behavior modification. *Journal of Abnormal Psychology* 78(1):107-126.

67. Osborn, A. F. 1963. *Applied Imagination: Principles and Procedures of Creative Problem Solving*, 3rd ed. New York: Charles Scribner's Sons.

68. McKay, M., M. Davis, and P. Fanning. 1995. *Messages: The Communication Skills Book*, 2nd ed. Oakland, CA: New Harbinger Publications.

69. Freeman, A., J. Pretzer, B. Fleming, and K. Simon. 1990. *Clinical Applications of Cognitive Therapy*. New York: Plenum.

70. Meichenbaum, D. 1977. *Cognitive Behavior Modification*. New York: Plenum.

71. Bourne, E. J. 1995. *The Anxiety and Phobia Workbook*, 2nd ed. Oakland, CA: New Harbinger Publications.

72. Marlatt, G. A., and J. R. Gordon, eds. 1985. *Relapse Prevention: Maintenance Strategies in the Treatment of Addictive Behaviors*. New York: The Guilford Press.

73. Marlatt, G. A. 1996. Taxonomy of high-risk situations for alcohol relapse: Evolution and development of a cognitive-behavioral model. *Addiction* 91(Supplement):37-49.

Jeffrey C. Wood, Psy.D., specializes in cognitive behavioral therapy, biofeedback, and life skills coaching. He is author of *Getting Help* and coauthor of *The Dialectical Behavior Therapy Skills Workbook* and *Therapy 101*. Wood lives in Westchester County, NY. Visit him online at www.drjeffreycwood.com.

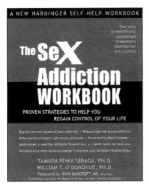

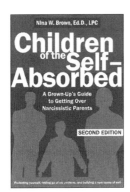

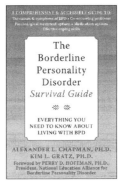